.50

M000317780

100
PSYCH

and a time to die

and a time to die

to die

Mark Pelgrin

Edited by Sheila Moon
and Elizabeth B. Howes

A RE-QUEST BOOK

THE THEOSOPHICAL PUBLISHING HOUSE
Wheaton, Ill., U.S.A.
Madras, India/London, England

First Re-Quest edition published by the
Theosophical Publishing House, Wheaton, Illinois,
a department of The Theosophical Society in America

Library of Congress Cataloging in Publication Data
Pelgrin, Mark, 1908 or 9-1956.
    And a time to die.

    (A Re-quest book)
    1. Cancer patients-Personal narratives. I. Title.
RC262.P4   1976. 362.1'9'699400924 [B]   75-26836
ISBN 0-8356-0305-9

Printed in the United States of America

*To all those
whose manner of dying
has enriched and illumined
the meaning of life*

For everything there is a season, and a time for every matter
  under heaven:
a time to be born, and a time to die;
a time to plant, and a time to pluck up what is planted;
a time to kill, and a time to heal;
a time to break down, and a time to build up;
a time to weep, and a time to laugh;
a time to mourn, and a time to dance;
a time to cast away stones, and a time to gather stones together;
a time to embrace, and a time to refrain from embracing;
a time to seek, and a time to lose;
a time to keep, and a time to cast away;
a time to rend, and a time to sew;
a time to keep silence, and a time to speak;
a time to love, and a time to hate;
a time for war, and a time for peace.

ECCLESIASTES 3:1–8.

Contents

Prologue

Every man is born and every man dies. None is born conscious of the significance of this birth in time, and most are unaware of the significance of this death. Some do have an intimation of the meaning of dying, and a few achieve an intensified relationship to the purpose behind the final life experience. Even fewer have ever chronicled the ways by which they came to that place where death seemed the ultimate step in self-fulfilment. This book is therefore a rare account, coming from a man who died at the age of forty-seven of cancer but who gave the last year of his life to a heightening and hastening of his search for all the seasons of God—a man who came, at the end, to where he could say yes to both sides of the paradoxes of Ecclesiastes.

Acceptance of the seasons of God is a task difficult to perform. Although a man sees the task as necessary—yes, even inevitable—although he knows with his mind that, as the prophet said, there is 'a time for every matter under heaven', he must be a staunch soul to bear the work of it. Into the purposes of the universe, it is not so hard to fit birth, laughter, love, peace. But weeping and war, casting away, death—these are more bizarre pieces to place in their season and time. This requires work and devotion and courage. And these Mark Pelgrin gave, with a sense of genuine meaningfulness, as he moved into the time and season of his death. He was neither 'good' nor 'selfless', as the world so absurdly judges these matters. He was, however, a truly religious man in the profound sense of the word. Life was to be lived 'under God', he thought—and so he lived life, sometimes soundly, sometimes unsoundly, always intensely. And he talked about it with himself. He wrestled with it and God in it. He hated it and loved it. Above all, he tried to find himself in it. This is what the book is about.

Mark Pelgrin did not write the book, but he wrote most of what is in the book, because he was a verbal man and was compelled, as some of us are compelled, to record in one fashion or another what went on in him. A few days before his death, when the idea of some time making use of his material was presented to him, he nodded and went on to more urgent things, the Word having by now passed beyond chronicling. But his copious scrawled notes do delineate his personal journey, most particularly the culmination of that journey. We have felt this to be of great relevance for many people, because when a man thus faces his 'time to die', he carries in his heart a universal confrontation and becomes an unintentional spokesman for all his brothers. The final mystery is not only his but ours, and we go with him, as we can, into his ultimate room. His meditations, sketches, letters, journal entries—these are markers on his way and on ours. Because he kept them at all, even if often in remarkable and almost illegible disorder, we are the richer. We are also the richer because he cared so absolutely, not only for his own outcome but for the outcome of his family and his contemporary world, and because he cared in a way which included the self—his self and other selves—and his God.

Who was this man? No one so very remarkable, judged from the outer facts of his life. He was a teacher, a husband, a father—Margaret, his first wife and mother of two children, died of cancer five years before his own death. He remarried, and his second wife, Ruth, also bore him two children. He never had either money or success in a worldly way. He sought for religious meanings in seminars on the Records of the life of Jesus—which seminars profoundly affected his orientation—and in extensive Jungian psychotherapy, and struggled always to deepen his self-knowledge. He loved; he was loved. In 1955 an operation led to a diagnosis of 'possible cancer', and until the spring of 1956 he wrestled with equivocal facts. Then cancer came, and he died.

No one very remarkable, this Mark Pelgrin. His life, seen from one angle of vision, was tragic. Seen from another, it was a rich life because he was a man who tried to make sense out of the universe, a *truly religious man for whom wholeness was an achievement and not an easy gift. The paradoxical nature of the journey to find the Self became for him a central concern. The wonderful Ecclesiastes passage about a 'season' and 'a time for every matter under heaven' was a favourite of his, and he once typed it out for himself, covering it with scrawled notations. This single page, found crumpled up in his files, reveals much of what he felt about the psychological-religious way. He wrote: 'Religious way not easy . . . religious statement is paradox . . . Self is the wish to pass beyond ourselves as we now are. . . . "Whosoever shall seek to save his life shall lose it and whosoever shall lose his life shall preserve it" . . . single question: if we really acted upon this wisdom would our lives be any different? . . . growth does not occur without dissolution . . . comfort and safety defeat life . . . the nature of the universe is Paradox, with the Devil as the backside of immortality.' Pelgrin was intensely conscious of paradox, of limitation, of mortality and its impingement, and therefore this book is a record of the meaning of a life heightened and enhanced by the facing of death.*

Only that material has been included in the book which seemed to the editors to have the most direct bearing on Pelgrin's essential search. Very much more was available, for Pelgrin had a wide perspective of the world encompassing him. He was in no wise a narrow man solely concerned with his own fate. He revelled in nature. He could be absorbed in music. He could argue half the night about philosophy. His concern for good teaching methods was very central to him, and he did much work to document his ideas. He was by way of becoming a fine scholar and critic of American thought and social philosophy. And he often did what so many promise themselves but do not do—he wrote letters to newspapers, to senators, and representatives of government, urging or protesting various public policies. He dared to be unorthodox, to dissent from his peers and his fellow-members of the 'lost generation' by exploring and talking about the bypaths of depth psychology and spiritual experience. However, most of his notes on these concerns had to be laid aside in the editing.

In addition to Prologue and Epilogue, the book is in four parts. 'The Encounter' is his long and vivid account of his illness and first operation, and his reactions to the ominous possibilities suddenly there. 'The Way Life Looked' is an autobiographical section, made up from various of his writings which seemed to be relatively direct considerations of the actual events of his life in sequence. 'The

PROLOGUE

Inward View' contains notes and journal entries dealing more or less specifically with his personal Jungian analysis, and all the discoveries of himself resulting from that. The final section, 'The Larger Meanings', deals with his tremendous struggles with himself and with God to understand what was the meaning of this completely equivocal situation, when life and death were balanced on a pinpoint year of time. It includes prayers, meditations, journal, letters, in which he articulated his final sense of meaning and fulfilment.

The book has been edited, with the consent and assistance of Pelgrin's wife, by Dr. Sheila Moon and Dr. Elizabeth Howes, Jungian analysts, who knew him, who were related, one way and another, to both his families, and who followed his 'journey' for ten years. Dr. Moon was Pelgrin's analyst, and has written the Prologue, the Epilogue, linking statements, and short explanatory passages wherever the editors felt them to be necessary. Dr. Howes was leader of the Records seminars referred to by Pelgrin, as well as his close friend.

All names in the text have been changed to preserve anonymity for those who may wish it so. As editors, we can only express our hope that this book may be no cause for stumbling to anyone, and may be a source of renewed trust that every human life can be a testament.

I

The Encounter
June 1955

———◆———

THERE IS probably much self-pity in this. There may be some
hint of courage. There is no opera or melodrama. In an encounter
of this kind one cannot afford to be dishonest with one's self.
Here is no place for heroics. I simply feel the urge to set it down,
as it happened, for it can only happen once in a life's time, except
that final end when the end is the beginning and the beginning is
the end. But that is a story that won't be written.

Before recalling the point in my illness when it became evident
that I must have a serious operation, on that sunny June afternoon talking to the surgeon, I find I must first briefly recount a
long-buried childhood memory and then a premonitory dream.
The memory of my first encounter with the shadow, the stub-
born fact of death in the universe, an April morning in the back-
yard of our house . . . I must have been ten or eleven at the time.
The shadow was represented in the form of our household pet, a
bright brown-eyed little spaniel whom we called Major Fuzzy.
He had been poisoned and he was lying in the spring grass, over-
arched by the two gnarled pear trees that dominated the yard,
and all the life had gone out of him. The stubby tail no longer
wagged. The imploring brown eyes were closed. The body was
bloated. And from the corpse there seemed to emanate a sweet,
cloying odour.

We buried him in the upper corner of the yard, where the old
chicken-house used to be, and I remember carving a little cross

I

for him. But, curiously, that sweet odour persisted for many weeks and it appeared again the following spring. For two years I was puzzled by this curious relationship between a sweet odour and a dead dog, until I stumbled one day upon the answer. Of course! There was no connection. I had taken a lilac bush that bloomed with scented fragrance in April, and associated it with Fuzzy's death. 'April is the cruellest month.' Perhaps it is no accident that Walt Whitman's 'When Lilacs Last in the Door-yard Bloom'd' has as its key symbol, the connecting of Lincoln's death with April lilacs. Every leaf of a lilac is a miracle, for Walt, and the connection of Major Fuzzy and the lilac scent expresses the miraculous way in which life and death are interwoven, fused, paired, one in the other.

The dream, which occurred the Saturday night of Easter vacation (the night before Easter Sunday and twenty-four hours before the rash that suddenly appeared on my skin and was the beginning of my illness), was of the death of my first wife Margaret. She had, in fact, died of cancer five years before. Con-sciously, I did not know then what was to happen to me. For two weeks, I had had 'just a rash', an uncomfortable rash. In fact, my doctor sent me to a skin specialist, whose office, he said, was the Elysium for all itches and rashes. Two weeks later the skin man suddenly looked at my eyes and remarked, 'You've got jaundice.' Now jaundice, of which there are many kinds, is simply a manifestation of a liver disorder. What kind of jaundice? One, certainly, I was to learn, that carried with it a terrible and potent itch. Itch is pain, or, rather, just below the threshold of pain. The itch was to stay with me, get worse and worse in its insistent 'bite' upon the skin, from Easter Sunday until the operation, and, more mildly; for several weeks after, when the jaundice disappeared.

I can't begin to interpret the dream of my wife's death, but it remains so vivid I set it down here, like the Bile Dragon that I must also bring in before we meet the surgeon. I am not sure whether this curious monster appeared out of a dream or out of a half-conscious state of semi-wakefulness but he became so clear as an image and so ever-present that I am sure he was dredged up out of deep layers within, like a Protean sea-serpent emerging from the sea at its lowest depth. Perhaps he was a satisfactory way of accounting for my itch. The itch came from within, from excess bile in my blood-stream, and there was little I could really do with it on the surface. Ice-packs, salve with a mild anaesthetic, brought temporary release, but not much.

My dragon was quite unconventional. He had no tail. He had no eyes to hypnotize one. He had no mouth. He breathed no fire. He was a silent, undulating, long piece of greenish flesh, sometimes with red veins, and from this undulating snake-like thrust of flesh there stood out stiffly, like bristles on a brush, innumerable hairs. Sometimes these would undulate with the monster, tickling my nerve-ends. Other times, the flesh would undulate and the bristles would be stiff, upright. If there is a hell for me, I am sure it is peopled with Bile Dragons.

Now let me return to the surgeon's office. For two and a half months we had explored every other possibility. I had come to talk business. The last recourse was an operation.

Moments of dramatic import in one's life are moments in which the observation is sharp with detail. The office was on a second floor, directly across from the hospital where I was to go a few days later. The street at this point was lined with large old sycamores, some of them a half-century old. The fog on the coast brought a stiff afternoon breeze and I recalled the bright green leaves dancing in the wind and the hum of traffic floating up from the highway, and the intense blue of the sky, and the silence there between us, the surgeon at the other side of the desk, a row of books along the side, by a blotter. We both lighted up cigarettes. The most prominent book had a reddish-brown colour with gold-leaf lettering: 'Cancer.'

'Don't be alarmed,' he said, as he caught me looking at the title. He took it up and thumbed through for a page or two. 'This is all I have to illustrate what we need to know here. It just happened to be here. Now, let's see. I will draw you a sketch. Here is the pancreas and this duct leads to the liver and this to the duodenum, or little intestine. . .'

The silence became more intense for suddenly I realized this was Jehovah speaking. This was the man who contained in himself the words that would make my future intelligible or unintelligible. Jehovah in this case was really a very fine man and a very, very skilful surgeon. He was tall and fortyish, with a handsome, classical face, almost like Hermes. But there was a mask he wore perpetually. No matter how kindly your disposition,

3

when you are a surgeon, I imagine, when you are close to the secrets of the vital organs of a patient, when you are on intimate terms with the twitch of the nerve and the heave of the blood, your only protection is a mask, or you would lose what you have of skill and integrity. You cannot be God and you must be careful of what you say. Very careful.

He was being careful. He first recalled the previous stages. At first, he and his associates had clung to the hypothesis that I had hepatitis, or inflammation of the liver, but the tests made did not indicate my jaundice fitted that diagnosis. But we would try it. I had crept home from classes unwillingly and gone to bed. I had spent weekends in bed. For the only cure here was rest. Moreover, I had insisted on finishing my teaching year, and finals had been over by two weeks. I had been in the hospital for five days, for observation. They had taken a biopsy, that is, reached in with a tiny instrument and secured a piece of my liver. There was no indication of cirrhosis, or degeneration of the cells. All they could discover was that the bile ducts were enlarged. And the bile was being diverted, in some unaccountable way, into the blood-stream.

'Now,' he continued, 'we are ready for an exploratory operation and we will find one of three things. Let me give it to you in terms of percentages. Percentagewise, there is a seventy-five per cent chance you have a stone. Now seventy per cent of these stones are lodged in the duct from the pancreas to the small intestine and this seventy per cent lodge and dislodge.'

'You mean they kind of bob up and down?'

'Yes. To put it that way. Sometimes the bile gets through to the right place and sometimes it doesn't. This is not so in your case.' (I could see he was working hard on these percentages.) 'If it is a silent stone, as we call it, yours is part of the thirty per cent that lodge solidly and we can remove it.'

'Yes, go on. . . .'

'All right. There is a twenty per cent chance of a tumour. There could be a benign tumour somewhere, pressing against the duct. And. . . .'

'Malign?' I was persistent.

'Yes. In the pancreas. Cancer in the pancreas. Now I only tell men these things, you understand. Never women. But men need to know.'

4

I nodded, frightened. Of course, men have jobs. They must plan for the future. Not so important for women. Men have courage. Women don't need to know.

'What about the percentages here?'

'About twelve-and-a-half of each, malign, benign, and the silent stone, of course. Now you will be in the hospital ten days more or less. You should go in two days before to rest before the operation. The operation will be this coming Saturday. In the morning. I will arrange for a room.'

'Thanks, Doctor.'

Well, thanks, Doc. I drove home in a cloud of figures. $12\frac{1}{2}$... $12\frac{1}{2}$... 75 ... 70% of the 75. It was like a call-board on the stock market. And that night a curious little picture sequence formulated in my mind. Indeed I even almost forgot about the Bile Dragon. The silent stone bobbed up and down in the duct and became a merry little thingumajig, dancing in tea-kettle frenzy. I could even see it removed and held in my hand. I have no idea what a 'silent stone' is, in medical terms. I am not really too curious about the organs and their ailments in me, as far as details and scientific terms go. That job is up to the surgeon. My job is to reconcile his facts with my spirit. So that stone, lying there in my hand, was round, green like jade, a kind of lovable keepsake. The benign tumour became a red thumb, friendly little fellow, pressing gently on a duct. The malignant tumour was an evil white swirl, for the shadow is white sometimes, circling around a dark splotch, jelly-like, with a dark centre, at war with me, discordant, a Walter Piston chord suddenly interrupting the flow of a Beethoven Pastoral Symphony.

Except for colds, 'the flu,' and two or three minor childhood ailments I had never been really ill before. I had been in hospitals for others, but never for myself, not counting the biopsy five days two weeks before. Institutions are organized around a purpose, the school for education of the young, a museum to study and enjoy objects of the past, a political party to get votes and win elections. A hospital is organized around the dismal fact of human malady. The nurses whisper in the hallways. A cry is sometimes heard in the night. But the rooms are sealed off, one from the other, and I was in a private room rather than a ward, a fact for which I was later very grateful. When you are very ill you need to be very alone with your illness, even though it costs more. A ward is good when you are rapidly recovering and need to talk to others. So I could only guess those two days and two nights before the operation as to the myriad sicknesses that had brought all of us, in our separate cubicles on the second floor, to a building that was unified around one purpose, 'There goes a sick person.'

In some ways, the suspense before an operation is more deadly than the discomfort afterwards. I still had my Bile Dragon, who trailed across my sleeping and waking consciousness. Sometimes I referred humorously to him as Mr. Mannaluke, just why I don't know. Manna is life food and Luke is the author of one of the Synoptic Gospels and maybe I was trying to befriend the little monster. Most of all I was afraid, especially when I rattled off those percentages, like beads on a rosary. It is fear of the unknown that plagues us. I wanted the thing settled. It is fortunate I am a reader. I could drug myself with books, and almost for an hour at a time forget that I existed. In addition to some short stories and a novel, I found that Lilian Smith's *The Journey* was very helpful. As I am a very rapid reader, I read more books those two days than I had all during the school year. Prayer, meditation, contemplation didn't seem to work. I was too anxious.

As the Time approached, I was acutely aware of floating in the ceiling, watching myself on the bed below. A nurse came in and gave this creature down there a shot, to cause the blood to coagulate. Another nurse came in and gave a shot to start the anaesthesia. Then came the house doctor, both nurses, and some boy, who fumbled with the bed-rail. The gurney was placed against the bed and I was rolled over upon it. Then this person down there was pushed out of the room, into a hall, into an elevator. We ascended two floors. I was still, figuratively, in the ceiling. But I climbed back into myself when we entered a large room and now I was getting very, very sleepy. There were large windows, and whispered voices, and I was in a Renaissance palace, with huge wall hangings, and a mural, like the Sistine Chapel, with huge distorted pictures, with perspectives fading into perspectives.

Later I learned I had been 'under' almost all day. The operation had lasted nearly four hours. The bill from the hospital indicates that I was given about forty dollars' worth of blood transfusion, whatever amount that is. When I awakened, Ruth

6

was holding my hand. How warm she felt! How good to see her! Sure I was going to live, for her. I was still pretty drowsy, because I went back to sleep again, comforted. When I wakened once more, it was dark. This time the surgeon was standing to my right. I made tentative discoveries with my eyes and hands. A tube, it seems, ran down the back of my throat from what was evidently my stomach, through my nose, and out along the bed to a jar on my left. With a sharp awareness, I came awake. Self-preservation is the first law of life. The office visit became crystal-clear. The thingumajig merrily bobbing up and down. Had it been removed? Or was it. . . .

'Well,' looking directly at the surgeon, 'was it. . .'

His impassive face seemed to say, 'Must you ask now . . . must you ask now?'

'Well?'

'There goes your silent stone. It wasn't that.'

'Well?'

'It was cancer. I would diagnose it as that. Funny. I took biopsies and have just had the report. No cancer cells there. There is a tiny chance that it might be pancreatitis, inflammation of the pancreas, but what I saw looks like cancer. Indeed, I would diagnose it at that. So did the house doctor with me. We both looked. Still. . . .'

I closed my eyes. The anxiety was over, no matter what the result. I knew. There was no unknown. All was known. Lightning strikes twice. Events come in twos. I had been all through this with Margaret five years before. Now I must go all through it myself. Of course, one tiny, tiny sunlit ray of hope. But I must press on. I must know.

'How long?'

'How do you mean?'

'When will IT come back?'

'For this kind? One, two years, maybe eighteen months. You are on a year-to-year basis.'

All right. All right, then. The surgeon left and Ruth came in. I was fully awake and alive now. How wonderful to see her. She knew. So we talked. He had just seen her and commented on the strange little ray of hope in the cancerless biopsy. But he was too terribly clear otherwise. 'I would diagnose it as cancer.' Was this all a fib? Was he leaving me one hope to go on? The backbone of our species, *homo sapiens*, is stiffened by hope, one of the most essential human ingredients. We talked of people we had heard of who had been diagnosed as having an 'incurable disease' and who had lived for years after the doctor's edict. We talked of the relative nature of life and time. Some people live to be eighty or ninety without ever having realized the fullness of themselves. I had one good year ahead, at least. What was I worrying about? How lucky to have had the summer seminar experiences in psychology and religion! It was like having a bank, upon which one could draw credit, little techniques to make life richer, ways of accepting the opposites, the good-evil, hope-terror paradox of the universe. Why, a year could be spun out into a decade. Why be limited by time and space? It isn't how long you live but what you do with what you have. God's will be done. God has nothing to do with shortness or lengthiness of life. To reverse a physical fact would be to reverse Himself, for He must be bound by his own natural laws. Then I fell asleep.

It would be nice to say that I held to this mood of acceptance all through my stay at the hospital, that with courage and strength, with my chin erect, I 'took it on the jaw'. There were other times when, as I phrased it to myself, I 'whistled up my courage'. I was proud to be a man. I was loved by my family. People respected and liked me. The phone calls, and notes, and letters that poured in attested to that. Some were from my students. This pleased me. People were concerned. It is only when you are ill that you know how many, many friends you have. The doctor dropped in often, those days. He had told Ruth I was an 'extraordinary guy'. We talked philosophically. 'Yes,' I said, 'it doesn't matter whether we are talking about the Old Testament "I am who am" or the New Testament "Thy will be done" or the "Facts are . . ." of you scientists. It all amounts to the same thing. You can't change it tomorrow. I have IT. The test is what I do with what I have.'

It would be nice to say these thoughts remained permanently, but I am no hero, and very human. The opposite was true. Every conceivable kind of human emotion and mood swept through me, like tides in subterranean caverns.

The day that followed the operation, I became intently aware of the equipment around me. The humming sound, I discovered,

8

came from a tiny motor in the jar that drained from the tube that ran through the nose to the stomach. The idea here was to keep the stomach juices in flow and pumped so I would not vomit. Vomiting would endanger the 'adjustments' the surgeon had made inside. The main adjustment, I learned, was to move the duct away from the inflamed area and put it in a healthy area. (What delicate skill such a surgery!) The half-gallon bottles of liquid, on the other side of me, hanging from a kind of metal cross-tree, were for intravenous feeding. The vein in my right arm was pricked and it took from two to four hours for the drip drip of the bottle, with its life-giving minerals and vitamins, to feed my blood. It was not until the fourth day that I was able to taste a little jelly and drink some tea. The sensation was like that of enjoying a delicious Christmas dinner. Every bite of food was a thanksgiving. And the tube from the bandage across my abdomen was to draw off excess bile from the organs within to another jar, to my left. This I was to keep with me for nearly two weeks. When it was at last pulled out, four days after I was home, I felt my umbilical cord with the hospital had been cut.

The hospital room was plain, the nurses kind, but the most meaningful spot for concentration was the window, framed outside by a sycamore tree, of which a single branch, heavy with bright green leaves, swayed in the wind and glittered in the sun. How wonderful the world of colour and motion! Perhaps this life we live now is paradise, particularly just being, watching the leaves of a sycamore. Sometimes they were yellow-green, sometimes blue-green. At sunset, they reddened. When the wind blew, they danced like little fairies, and each leaf was different, each had a personality of its own. One tall leaf was motionless while three or four small leaves seemed to dance around it. When I forgot myself, lost in the miracle of the leaves, I was contented, absorbed. From such absorption I was wakened by human consciousness, by memory, which is future as well as past, by the sudden strange turn of my journey in life, by the anxieties of a time and space-conscious being. With this awareness came the adversary. Sometimes I found myself talking aloud with him, disputing, arguing, imploring. He was formless. I could not visualize this creature. But he was really there, this part of me that held a dialectic with the other part.

'What an unfortunate thing to happen, just when the twins

9

are two years old. I will never see them grow up. They needed a father, their own father. Why couldn't you have waited, at least until they were in school, or for a time at least? They will never know me. Can't you hear?'

'Sure. Face the facts. I can't change them. How do you know they won't fare well? Maybe. . . .'

'Look! I am not playing a role in *The Bridge of San Luis Rey*. You can't argue that all the threads of my life have been wound to the point that it is the best time for me to leave now. Not at all. Look! I am not thinking of myself, see? Here, for the first time in my life, my salary has got to the point—that point you understand is one of the highest school-teacher salaries in this state—where, once we pay off a few more bills, we will be on easy street. I mean we will have a little extra and not be in the red all the time. Ruth needs that money. The children need that money. Now Ruth will have to go back and work on minimum school-teacher's wages, peon wages, and this will be awful hard on her.'

'Aren't you regaling yourself with the future, though! How you revel in believing you are cheated . . .'

'Of course I am cheated, God damn you. I have looked to a sedate retirement. I want to see John and Eric go through college. I had enough of this with Margaret. Surely you could have granted me something more. I'm no thing. I'm a man, and an upright one. Sure, I've been clumsy. But I've done a lot of good for my students. I am known as one of the best teachers at the college. And I was on the threshold of a new maturity, a new self-discovery. Just recently I have learned to give inspirational talks that wowed my audience. I could be useful to you, YOU, don't you understand, for another decade or two.'

'Sure . . . but maybe you've brought this all on yourself.'

'That's what Job's friends told Job. Remember Bildad, and Eliphaz, and Sophar, how they sat by the dungheap for three days silently? They were good friends of Job. But they carried an old primitive idea that retribution is given by God directly in this life, that we prosper when we have God's favour, and that we are cast down when we lose His favour. He does these things when we don't perform the proper ritual. Very well, this past year I leaned too much to the right side of me. I taught two evenings a week, belonged to too many committees, tried to do too much. I gave no time to what I needed most, quiet beingness. I was always in an extrovert hurry. I was lopsided, vertical. I should have corrected it sooner. And I tried to drown my rash, that first two weeks before I discovered jaundice, by drinking a lot of wine before I went to bed. But this was excusable. I wanted to sleep hard and overcome the itch. Anyway, don't make me a victim of primitive superstition. Human consciousness has gone beyond that. I did NOT bring it upon myself.'

'Very well, have it your way.' A cunning fellow, this one.

Who was it told me once: 'Little boys don't cry!' Or does one cry when one is ready, and I was never really ready? I had cried for Major Fuzzy those distant years back to the backyard garden and the lilac scent. When I couldn't sleep, during the jaundice itch, there were some choke-sobs. Long before Fuzzy the presence of the shadow had surrounded me, in vivid form, as I suddenly recalled it. A forgotten flash of memory had been evoked by the Adversary.

I am seven and we are living in a tiny apartment above a drugstore in the mining camp. We had come to the high dry plateau of South America . . . because of my mother's health, 'Your mother is dying.' She had had three mastoid operations, the result of an infection she had acquired as a child of seven, during one hard, cold winter. Exposure by an ignorant nurse, I was told. It is midnight, my mother is groaning, and my father is wringing his hands. 'She is dying, she is dying.' The doctor comes. My mother is fighting for her breath. A chill wind, sweeping down from the mountains beyond the copper-smelter, rattles the tarpaper of the roof and whistles around the corners. I must have been very frightened, but I don't remember crying.

I am eight. We still live in the same apartment. Three days before, a detachment of bandits had raided the town, removed gold from the bank vault, stolen some dresses from the department store, even put a few bullets in the brick wall of the drugstore building in which we lived. Now three men had been caught by police. In traditional custom, they were strung up from a pipeline that crossed a cut in the hill, where a road led from town to the American settlement and the American school. This grisly event took place five blocks from our apartment and the only way to school was directly under these men. A gaping crowd filled the street. The three hanging fellows were short, their tongues bloated, their lips blue-pale. 'Little boys aren't afraid.'

So that morning I passed under them to school and that afternoon I passed under them again for home. But I didn't cry.

But now the Adversary was gone. Perhaps he was, like Satan in Job, gone from the business with me to the business with others. 'And the Lord said unto Satan, Whence comest thou? Then Satan answered the Lord, and said, From going to and fro in the earth, and from walking up and down in it.' For a moment I hovered on the verge of tears. Then the walls came down, like Jericho, and it seemed as though I cried for hours and hours. Little boys MUST cry for crying is a kind of prayer. Crying is catharsis. 'I will drown myself in tears,' I told myself, my back on the bed, my hands and eyes imploring the vacant ceiling.

I started by crying for myself. Woe, oh woe. I cried for tiny little incidents my imagination envisioned, delights in the future of which I had been robbed. Eric with his college diploma in his hand, the ceremonies just over. Ruth taking a picture. His girl, perhaps, smiling and beaming and holding his hand. John poring over books in the University library. A senior. He has found himself, this one. Our garden, five years from now, a sunny July day, and the perfection of which I had made it. Flowers I would plant here. The barbecue would go there.

Then I moved up a step. I cried for Ruth. It would be so hard on her. She would have to shoulder burdens that could not be expected of so lovely a creature as that. I'll say one thing. I trusted in her courage. Ruth comes of strong stock. Must be the Mormons. She could take it. But I cried for her.

The walls were down and my inwards seem to dissolve completely when I thought of Margaret. I had never really cried for her before. I had tried to do my best but I had never been inside of her. Now I was miraculously transported inside her. There were tears of regret . . . 'if only' tears. I could have talked with her. I wanted her back to talk with her. But then I was tongue-tied. I did not know what to say. I could have rubbed her back every night, as the nurses did for me, but it had never occurred to me then that little acts of comfort of this kind would have more meaning than what I thought was my courageous 'facing up to reality' . . . my getting of the meals, my cleaning the house, taking care of the boys, and too remotely administering to her needs. I bought the phonograph for her and the records.

But this was selfish. She would have enjoyed more the simple back rub. Two human beings in close and loving contact.

Then I cried for the human race, for everyone like us. For the man, whoever he was, in the room next door. For the watchman I remember reading about in the paper who was caught on top of a flaming tank of wine and who jumped screaming into the boiling fury. For the strange accidents described in *The Cruel Sea*, the torpedoed tanker, the burning oil chasing the desperate swimmers. For Michelangelo, who died at 87, and for Thoreau, who died at 37. And for my friends, and the children, and all of us caught in the web of human experience. And I felt I was inside each of them.

All right, then, the more one is conscious the more one is sensitive to sorrow and pain and woe, as well as to joy, and content, and even ecstasy. So I cried for the many joyful moments I have known. And the female ctenophore I read about in the *New Yorker*. The microscopic males of this tiny species circle the female. They whirl madly. One finally reaches her, in a frenzy, and she is fertilized. But she dies immediately. In the act of intense life, of birth, she dies. The only species of its kind known to exist. I had passed, in a brief time, through three stages of prayer—low prayer, which is petitionary, middle prayer, which is intercession on behalf of others, and high prayer, identification and willingness to cooperate with a higher consciousness than self. The walls had tumbled down. The wild wide intuitive reach of time and space, lost now, always forever lost to all of us, had been placated. This mood I could not hold for long. It was too intense. But the problem that remained had been highlighted. I must strike some kind of harmonious balance between the now and the thought of the future, between present and past. I would oscillate between the NOW and the FUTURE. I could not prevent this. But somehow I must learn, painfully perhaps, which of me belonged to the one and which to the other.

And I here discovered what Ruth and I called the 'sealing off' of ourselves. Something in us seals us off against pain and fear and anxiety about the future, blunting the edge of onrushing time. The dishes must be washed. Work must be done. A leaf must be studied. A rose must be enjoyed. The life of the present carries us on. Let the future take care of itself. This sealing is healing. To be a human being is to live on pluck, on faith in what we are doing right now as part of faith in the grand design. For most of us much of the time the dishes have to be washed and the meal prepared and if it were not this way we would have all gone crazy way back there at the outset when the first primate dropped from a tree and acquired consciousness and memory and awareness of himself in time and space and the pluck to endure it.

Something to put you to sleep puts you too hard asleep, so it is difficult to struggle with writing down your dreams. I was conscious in the hospital that I was dreaming a great deal. Inside, many things were going on, after the walls came down, and I only regret I could not get more than a few fragments. Two days passed. I began to read again. The jelly and tea for a day or two led to toast and tea and then finally to small light breakfasts and dinners. Every meal was like Christmas. The sycamore tree became more and more a marvel. Why look for miracles? Everything around us is a miracle. But it wasn't always that easy. 'I will show you fear in a handful of dust.' That line from 'The Wasteland' also stuck in my consciousness, although the itching began to disappear and old Mannaluke became more and more like a friendly dog. Soon he was to go away, like some stray pet, possibly to haunt some other fellow somewhere. Or was he just dormant? Let sleeping dogs lie!

I did remember a few very revealing dreams, though. Thursday night, five days after the operation, I dreamed I was in a room with two doctors. One was like the surgeon, a modern expert, the true scientist. The other was a crude little guy who kept arguing with the surgeon about the need for what he called 'home cures'. I was very ill, in this dream, and they were talking quietly but intensely over me. Sometimes we were all standing in swamp water. There were crocodiles about but I did not know what to make of these Behemoths. They didn't really terrify me. Indeed, they seemed to be friends of the ugly little doctor with his crazy talk about 'home cures'. I was shaping a piece of wood, trying to let a figure buried in the wood come out. What it was, I didn't know. A crocodile? Or me?

Saturday morning I wrote down another dream. Again the incidents were vague and I was not sure, from my rough pencillings, that I was doing right by it. I dreamed I was on an arid hill, rising from a plain, not unlike the red-rock dry, cactus-strewn hills of the mining camp of my childhood. Another boy and I were pretending we were miners, that we were discovering or were about to discover another great Comstock Lode. There were other boys there and we were very excited in our play and there was talk of diamonds. What fun to discover diamonds! We ran past the old schoolhouse, with its dilapidated boards, up a dry canyon. My companion and I left the others and found ourselves alone on a high plateau. Diamonds and gold were strewn everywhere. I yelled, 'Look. Look. The Koh-i-noor. It is as rich as that.' He yelled, too. I tried not to interpret this dream when I awoke, but I did set down simply: 'To be all I haven't been.'

My last dream in the hospital was about a need to find some rich oriental tapestries to illustrate my work in literature to a class. They belonged to an Armenian family and particularly to a girl in this family. I was going with her in a canoe and we crossed a stream. I went back to get her family, as we all had to go across. We carried these brocades or tapestries with us, but they fell in the stream and were partly spoiled. The girl and I realized they must be repaired. But to do this we had to canoe upstream to a hidden cave, just the two of us, and this was hard. We made several unsuccessful tries. Again I tried not to interpret, but Ecclesiastes came to mind. 'A time for sorrow, a time for joy,' and the marvellous ring of those tremendous lines. There was a time for everything, teaching and tapestries, lost caves upstream, and all opposites had to be sewn together and all things renewed.

So the encounter properly ended when I found myself deliciously in the car, deliciously Ruth at my side, deliciously home with the children, deliciously in the garden. Lovely, lovely, lovely, I told myself. The world was bright with new promise. I had read about different kinds of heavens and hell. Dante had a hell, a heaven, a purgatory. I liked the five stages of heaven in Hinduism. I could go into describing that for hours. And there was a lot to say for just delicious being. But this mood was short and there would be other times when the sun would darken.

We are seeds on the way to the moon. Perhaps someday we will fly to the moon. It isn't important whether we get there or not. It is important that we aspire to get there. Not the physical moon. But that eternal symbol of something just beyond our consciousness that illuminates us now and then and gives us hope of getting a little nearer. Like each leaf outside the hospital window, each seed is different from every other. We must watch our seeds and rescue them. But the dishes have to be done, the meal prepared. Faith and hope and courage are really not block-buster words. They are something we live by as we sweep our house in the morning.

II

The Way Life Looked

———◆———

The 'encounter' with the Adversary precipitated Mark Pelgrin into an unbelievably accelerated stage of his journey toward the Self. But this journey had begun long before his final encounter. Intimations of it are evident even in some of his youthful romantic writings; and as early as 1947, when he was first made aware of the meaning and value of self-knowledge, he was beginning to articulate this sense of journeying. He said it and mused on it over and over during the next years, ever re-examining the events of his life in their relevance to this major concern.

Before Pelgrin says how these events looked to him, what were were some of their factual realities? Mark Pelgrin was born of middle-class parents in a middle-sized American city. He was an only child. In his early childhood his family moved to a small Latin-American village where his father worked for an American corporation, and where Mark was virtually cut off for several crucial years from any normal relationship with a peer group. Here he lived much of the time, as he said, in a 'fantasy world' of heroic deeds of valor until the family returned to the United States and to the city of his birth. Grammar school and high school, as he experienced them, were wretched memories. He was plagued by acne, was painfully isolated vnd shy, and thought of himself as 'muddling Mark'. Toward the close of his high school years he began to compensate for his sense of inferiority by becoming the 'clown'. He also became the piano-playing member of a jazz band, which occupation helped him to put himself through college. It also provided an outlet for pent-up emotions. From then on, he genuinely appreciated good jazz, in addition to his sensitive and perceptive response to symphonic and chamber music. In high school, too, he served as editor of school papers and literary publications, and thus started his long years of interest in writing.

Pelgrin said that his first year of university work remained forever sharp in his remembrances because of what he described as 'my attempts to compete in writing with people far better than I in this gift'. After a year or so, acting on the advice of a favourite professor, he decided to be a 'critic and scholar'. When he had received his bachelor's degree from the university he entered the teaching profession. Shortly thereafter, he married.

Although she is not the central personality in this chronicle, Margaret, Pelgrin's first wife, who also died of cancer, was an unforgettable individual with a major influence on his destiny. There were, to be sure, many ups and downs, many low moments and difficult times in their twelve years of marriage, as both were complicated persons actively going out to meet their fates. But she had a truly friendly relationship to her inner world of dream and fantasy, despite her oftimes stormy effect on her outer environment. Mark wrote of her: 'The impossible that is the subject of fairy tale, she believed, was the probable of our unconscious. . . . Her life she saw as a personal fairy tale, and the warning bell that was set off by cancer initiated a profound quest for the discovery of self, a subjective journey from which she drew a germinative power akin to that which so many sensitive people have drawn from the fairy tale.'

During this marriage, lasting from 1936 until Margaret's death, Pelgrin first taught high school in a small town, then in a state college, and finally in a junior college. Margaret and Mark had two children, and living was not easy, finances difficult. Summer vacations were spent camping in the high mountains which Mark loved throughout his life. Margaret eventually took a job so that Mark could work for his doctor's degree. And then in 1945 she had an operation for cancer, shocking both of them into a terrible awareness of the transitoriness of life, of the deep need for an increased self-fulfilment. They began reading in the field of depth psychology, especially the work of Dr. Fritz Kunkel and Dr. C. G. Jung, and began to see a relationship between inner and outer existence.

Two years after his wife's operation, the two of them attended a summer seminar to study the life and teachings of Jesus, as found in the Synoptic Gospels. This seminar, concerned with trying to cut through the accretions of Christian dogma to permit the actual words of the man Jesus to come into focus, gave both Mark and Margaret a new sense of religious meanings. Mark returned to similar seminars during the following years, feeling that for the first time he understood a religious Way as legitimate and possible. These seminars, and the ideas behind them, provided a change of direction and a recovery of values lost in the wilderness of the Twenties, the futility of two World Wars, the failure—for him, at any rate—of orthodox Christianity. As a modern disbeliever, he found that there could be meanings to 'losing the life' and to 'the Kingdom of God'.

Before Margaret died, she began work in Jungian analysis, giving herself wholeheartedly to it until the very day of her death. Her last recorded dream was of a small island in the sea, with a dark man seated there braiding strands of bread. He looked up and said, 'The light and the dark must be braided together'. And it was so with each of them, that the light and the dark were brought together, for Mark, too, entered analysis and continued off and on during the next years, with complete involvement for his last year.

During his wife's final illness, and after her death, Pelgrin tried to be mother and father to his two children, as well as to teach. Then in 1950, Mark met Ruth and they were married shortly thereafter. Eventually two children were born to them, increasing the total family to six. Although there were the perennial problems of time and money to complicate happiness, there was yet much happiness. Very naturally, because of Mark's enthusiasm, Ruth attended seminars with him. She went into analysis. Life for them grew ever richer and more consciously rewarding. Mark was doing more writing, was increasingly outstanding on his faculty, and was even, out of his maturing spiritual awareness, giving unorthodox 'sermons' and lectures at a nearby church.

Five years after this second marriage, Mark was taken ill with jaundice. An operation led to a diagnosis of 'possibly pancreatitis, but probable cancer'. So began the last months, uncertain, fearful, challenging. They were months of labour—for his own self-knowing, as inclusive as he could make it, with the help of analysis; for his own self-expression, in poetry and prose; for his understanding of God and the seasons of God; for his final relationships with his wife, his four children, the small moments of every day. And in late

19

spring, eight months after the first operation and a week after a second and futile operation, Mark Pelgrin died.

As he wrote in his notebook at some point in the last year, 'All life is Religious Statement, but the problem of the phrase is, all Life is not Religious Statement; it is Life Statement. All Life is Life Statement.' Life Statement and Religious Statement had for many years been intertwined for Mark. He had once quoted from R. L. Stevenson's Aes Triplex, '. . . so it is the first part of intelligence to recognize our precarious estate in life, and the first part of courage to be not abashed before the fact.' Mark recognized his 'precarious estate' much before his impending death. He had the courage to desire and to work for change in himself, to be doggedly honest and unabashed in his laying bare of his life. He did not merely generalize about things, he specified.

And how did his life look to him?

FOUR JOURNAL EXCERPTS, 1951

The tow-headed boy that was I, the deviation from the others that was I, heavy-lipped, pale, thin, his long spidery arms flopping as he walks through town from school, comes rushing at me out of the past with great sadness. Little do I remember before then. My mother, gaunt, and as she said, 'dying', and my father at once fierce and tender, are ghost figures, shadows on the edge of the circle that circumscribed my nine-year-old experience. And what a circle bounded me! Our apartment was above the botica or drugstore, and I here discovered Tarzan and took off into imaginary nightplay. Below, south of the brick building, was a vacant sand lot with a dirty and smelly creek in which I played—sandplay that provoked ridicule on the part of the little boys and girls that stood and watched me.

Particularly I remember coming home from school one afternoon—or was it noon, for lunch? A sunny spring day with the high plateau winds blowing across the mountain desert. A black bag was slung on my shoulder and in the bag was a drawing pad and pencil. Every now and then I would take it out and pause and draw a sketch of a building. I was evidently trying to do a map of the town—or was I trying to single out attention? For the boys followed me, nodding their heads, and crying 'loco'. It is as though this boy is still walking inside me, as though he must be explained—and yet so difficult the explaining—the only child, isolated from the American part of the town where the other boys played, caught in the veiled secrets of his dream-world, and unable to deal with the real world around him! So sad that boy, so lonely, so searching for security, love—and above all, so very, very clumsy.

It is this little boy I shall have to work to find. What was he like? What image of himself did he have? Why? What meaning had this secret inner life for him?

The child is father of the man! The man got how he was, possibly, because the child had to clown to find his place with others. As an only child he had no relation with his parents, because they did not comprehend him. His own family were clowns. Their own clowning was unconscious—their humour a kind of fierce retaliation against something handed to them by their parents. Tossed out of this one-child sterile world, inadequate in athletics, a bookish person who lived in his own world of private fancy, he attempted relatedness either by (1) pretending to be a genius—which only worked with the gullible; (2) pretending to be a clown. The main point was to draw attention. Hence—that poor little distracted tow-headed kid of nine drawing a map of a Central American village as he walked down the street, the kids putting their hands to their heads and saying 'loco'. Hence—the dream escape of playing in the sand, of building cities in front of grown-ups or foreigners, who could only see this as very odd and funny. Loco! Hence his father's remark on a picnic, as all the people watched his attempts at creation on the sand: 'Well, I guess it's all right. Some older boys play in the sand.'

That little boy down at the end of the corridor who is calling to me—the tow-head at 9, 12, or 7—what values did he have?

*   *   *

The ugly duckling idea must begin early. For example, I got myself in the ridiculous position at age of eleven or twelve of being chased by tough girls with rocks. I was naturally afraid of them. The steam-roller was also a monster to me in those days. I would walk a mile of extra streets to get around a steam-roller. I never played games as a child. I did all I could to avoid athletic programmes and games, though I hiked much alone and with friends and got my bit of exercise that way. In Junior High I was thought ridiculous and queer. The validity of this was established when I wrote a history, in the 9th grade, about a bat-like strange creature in a dark inter-planet world. The English teacher read it out loud and told my mother at Boy Scout meeting that I was a genius. Nevertheless one of my family heard from a student that I was queer, and told this to my parents who relayed it back to me. (There is undoubtedly much of my mother in me, in vivacity, tactlessness, surface outward thinking, lacking in the inward comprehension of self. Quick flash, shallow moods, unstable and temperamental. I inherited the Victorian world, and the cliches of that period were constantly recited to me.)

*   *   *

We are what we are but we are also what we are not. What was omitted and unlived in life is as important for conscious assimilation as what was lived. It is now increasingly clear that I became in part what was unlived in my parents. Of course the particular pressures of the lower middle class to which they belonged influenced their behaviour and thus mine. I must, by all means, not come home with a 'mechanic's hands' but as some kind of 'white collar' worker, an educated, professional man, something 'big,' a writer, or lawyer, or doctor, or professor—something of that kind. I was not to work with my hands but with my head. All this pushed me out of my social class to another class, the 'intellectual,' and to four years of college, four years of graduate work, M.A., PH.D., academic kudos. My standards became those of the upper middle class, and by a tragic irony, in so reaching, I lost contact with my parents and the positive values they held.

My lived life became that of the intellectual 'bookman,' at home with history, philosophy, literature, culture. I had to leave out the non-intellectual side, competitive sports, tools, dealing with things; thus I sacrificed spontaneous, instinctual maleness, solidity, and a forthright and direct approach to reality, warm, unrehearsed.

In the 9th grade there was the pretty and somewhat striking English teacher who, on the basis of two grotesque Poe-like writing sketches of mine, told my mother I was 'a genius'. Another teacher 'discovered' me in the tenth grade and, through her, I took an active part in 'The Lit' and in writing features for the school paper.

On the other hand, some of the English students, because of

my feeble and unattractive attempts to court the girls, called me 'the snake'. The fact that I was an only child left me out on my own to establish identity, and had much to do, I think, with my awkward thrusts toward individuality. Originality I confused with eccentricity. I sought evidently to command attention, even if it meant playing the clown and the fool.

At the Junior College, where I first achieved that success and recognition with the group denied me in high school, I was made editor of the college paper. At the university, where after this literary success at Junior College I was again a little frog in a big competitive puddle, my first year was characterized by great emotional instability. I tried to write stories but they were very romantic efforts, childish and infantile things that could not compete at all with some of the extraordinarily good and realistic writing of some of the students. The other, earthy side of me, the playing of jazz in orchestras to earn my way through college, belonged to a world apart.

Once more a teacher 'saved me' in my senior year by giving mild praise to my critical writing. My two first themes for her were marked D minus. I went in to see her and she pointed out I was writing emotional 'fluff' and that she didn't care about the style—how I spent hours on the style!—but just the simple common-sense analysis of the literature I was assigned. Well, once I got the trick, my themes jumped up to a B. And, with her encouragement, I found myself shifting from my major in journalism—(I was going to be editor of a country newspaper) —to a major in literature. My career as a teacher was foregone. I took graduate work, particularly in her seminars, and first came into contact, in a deep sense, with the cultural history of the past, particularly the seventeenth and eighteenth century. Through her I recovered considerable sanity. My romantic temperament led me to play the Boswell to this dynamic individual. It was an excellent corrective, bringing new ideals of balance, common sense, rationality.

But the die had been well cast. I was to be over-cerebral about life. To be sure, all human beings have a predilection at birth. It is not quite the *tabula rasa* that Locke made it out to be. We are all strange combinations of the given and the acquired. I am pretty sure now I was a natural introvert, but my environment wrought in me an active, extroverted over-intellectuality. This was 'safe' for me, my invulnerable wall against hurts. To feel my way in a situation or through a situation would be too hard, for it would lead to awkwardness, a feeling of being ill at ease.

FOUR SKETCHES, WRITTEN IN 1955

Descending into the furnace heat of the valley from the cool of the Sierra early in September was like coming to the bottom of our wishes. Following my substitute year at the mid-state college we had cast our hopes in other winds. Perhaps another state college, or junior college, or even a high school nearer to 'civilization', we had hoped. I blanketed the state with application letters, but jobs were tight in teaching during those depression years, just as they were in other fields. The Union High School where I was to be was an outpost in the hinterlands, an unexpected and unwelcome detour in that road to success which is basic to the popular American belief in itself. In those days, we believed that the shortest distance between two points was a straight line that climbed upward to predetermined goals.

For people acclimated to the coastal region, the September heat was sinister. The ghostly white pyramid of a mountain hung upon the northern horizon like a cloud above the heat haze. The red and brown rocks of the foothills glistened in the fierce sun. A small town with many old houses, with roots going back to the forty-niner days when it was head of navigation on the Sacramento River and transfer point for the wagons that rumbled to the Shasta mines, the town baked in the tepid silence. The high school was at the edge of town, where the burned hills rolled in waves for miles back to the wild range on the west. There we met 'the boss', Principal Smith, a bald-pated fellow with blinking blue eyes who had held his job here for over thirty years. He gave us a list of available apartments and rooming houses in town. All of them dull, stuffy, mouldy.

I think Margaret and I got the idea at almost the same moment. If we are consigned to the country, why not live in the country? Before crossing the creaking bridge over the Sacramento River into town, we had passed through a little orchard and livestock area. Almond and peach orchards, interspersed by irrigated alfalfa fields, made it a kind of attractive oasis. We spent two days calling upon farmers and making ourselves acquainted with real estate agents. Yes, there was a cattleman who had forty acres in almonds, which were not paying anything that year. He had leased the crop to a neighbour and moved his family from his house to one in the high mountains, where he was 'running cattle'.

So our new habitation and our first experience in country life was an old California farmhouse, built somewhere in the 1890's, with high ceilings and nine rooms. Any one of the rooms, including the kitchen, would have been enough to hold a modern living room, dining-room, and bedroom. For heat there was a fireplace in the living-room, a small pot-bellied stove in the dining-room, and a huge wood range in the kitchen. In winter, we were to learn, the town became as cold as it was hot in summer. When our first baby, Eric, arrived in February, it was quite a chore even to keep at least these three rooms warm. The rest of the house we disregarded. We would both get up about 6.30 and start fires with manzanita wood, to which we would add oak. Two 'improvements' turned out to be our greatest disasters. A water heater, run by electricity, was supposed to give us hot water quickly. It did, but there was no instantaneous shut-off valve. Sometimes my young city bride would forget to shut it off and we would be reminded of approaching catastrophe only by the sound of hissing pipes and steam coming from the faucets. The water came from a well in back and was pumped to a leaky tank by an electric device that had also to be turned off by hand when the tank was full. Otherwise the water would run over, flood the mechanism, and burn out the motor. I will never forget Margaret's 'bad girl' look late one afternoon when I came home and found the tank had been running over all day. We split the cost with the owner. Or the bright and hot Saturday morning when I set out to burn a little pile of grass in back and nearly started a chain-fire that threatened house, barn, and half a dozen wheatfields. This was pioneering, we told ourselves, and that night had a fine orgy with some new friends of ours, whom I will call here the Peebles, and consumed nearly a gallon of sherry.

Bill Peeble and his wife, Lois, had moved in 'very important' circles at the university—fraternity, sorority, drama—but, like us, had been consigned to the hinterland. Bill liked to 'stick frogs', as he called it. That evening we drove out to the creek and, while the wives stayed in the car, noiselessly crept along the shore, brandishing flashlights, a sack, and spears. The big, fat bullfrogs hid in the reeds along the bank but every once in a while we would mesmerize one with our lights, stab it, and draw it out of the water, squirming, to stick in the sack. Margaret, sometimes over-delicate in such matters, wouldn't eat the fine mess of frog legs we cooked up afterward, but I do remember her listening intently to the conversation that followed. We were discussing our principal, whom Bill and I had nicknamed 'Bullet Bob'. Bill had asked me how I liked it.

'Fine,' I lied, because I was still somewhat queasy myself about frog-sticking.

'No, I mean working for old Bullet Bob.'

'I guess he is all right.'

'Sure. Lead eyes and kind of droopy. Especially when he sits on what I call the rubber pad. Second Period. He reads all the publisher's advertisements and just sits there. Nothing to do.'

'Well, he has been here a long time. Probably thinks he has everything running fine.'

'Listen . . . you must wait until Spring semester nears an end and we get to bargaining day.'

'What's that?' Margaret asked.

'You haven't heard? Well, the Unified School District, I should remind you, has less than 500 students, which means the California tenure law does not work here. Also there is no regular salary schedule. Now, unless you are lucky and get a call from the city—some nice spot—you've got to sign a contract for the next school year, right?'

'Right.'

'So now you get around nineteen fifty a year. Right?'

'Right.'

'About the middle of May each one on the faculty sneaks in for an interview with Bullet Bob to bargain for the next year. The coach, he'll come off best. This town loves football. The band man, he'll come off next best, maybe at twenty-eight hundred, because this town loves a band with its football. Of course, the agriculture teacher will get the highest salary.'

'What about English teachers?' Margaret cut in.

'Dime a dozen. That's what the Boss will say. A dime a dozen. You can pick them up anywhere. So why pay more?'

He was right, and for the three years I taught, as 'Head of the

English Department', I found myself in the unfavourable position of being an English teacher in competition with the far more valuable coach, band man, and 'ag' man. There was also the woman member of the board, who struck Norris's *The Octopus* off the library list because it 'libelled the Southern Pacific'. And the board member who spoke to the Boss about speaking to me about teaching socialism, the time we had a class discussion on public ownership of power. 'We are all socialists when we are very young, Mr. Pelgrin, but. . . .'

But, in retrospect, all this proved to be among the most fruitful of our experiences together. We learned the difference between small town and city life. In a small town, everyone knows everyone, including the skeletons in the family closet. One becomes acquainted with people that would otherwise be unknown—the chicken farmer, the sheep-herder, the PGE lineman. On the other hand, there is not the choice of friends that one can make in the city, for the metropolis is anonymous and out of the vast anonymity one selects those of his kind, those with whom he can be most easily convivial.

Like any public school, this high school revealed the social structure of the county through the magnification of adolescence. The town boys and girls, like their parents—except for the real old-timers—were closer to city ways. For the town was not rural in the older Middle Western sense of the word. Like all of the communities in the great Central Valley, its localism was disintegrating under the impact of industrialized, commercialized agriculture. The bank, the movie, the drug store, the grocery had become part of large California chains. Corporation farming, the leasing of orchards to the large packing companies, the dominant pressure of the Associated Farmers, was creeping into the county, as it had done years before in the San Joaquin Valley, and with it, labour strife. The farm kids, some of whom travelled thirty miles by bus to reach school, brought with them the pungent smells of the barnyard. Tucked in the hills nearby, there was even a remnant of hillbilly hog-acorn culture, the hogs eating the acorns around the front stoop, and Saturday night hoedowns, where everyone got drunk on 'corn likker' and old family feuds were inflamed into occasional knifings.

But, most of all, it was the country itself that held us. Swimming in the river on a hot May evening, the moonlight shimmering on the water and blanching the sand and stones white on the sandbar. Sunday jaunts to snowfields only two hours away, for skiing. Rambling hikes up the canyon, a wilderness of cliff and tumbling stream and oak and scrub pine as untouched by white men as it had been in the days of the Indians. Mounds of arrowheads. Or the Sacramento River, flooding over the plains in the great deluge of November, 1937, where our house, on a slight hill, was cut off from the rest of the world for three days. On our own place were fourteen orange trees, twenty almond, three pecan, two walnut, and a large persimmon. From the screened back porch, the view on a clear winter day, with the snow almost down to the foothills in the Cascades and the Lassen range, was breath-taking.

Margaret did not recover from Eric's birth quickly. And he was indeed an active baby. It took our combined energies to keep him from crawling into the fireplace or putting his arms around the red-hot pot-bellied stove in winter. We never saw one in our own yard, but this was good rattlesnake country and Eric's peregrinations outside in the yard kept us constantly on the alert. Although we confined ourselves to only a part of the big house, it was much too big to keep up. So I stumbled upon a task I gradually learned to enjoy, cooking the family meals, while Margaret wrestled with the old washer out on the screen porch or romped with Eric during the days when he was first learning to say 'Mama', 'Papa'.

We began to like people in what at first seemed an alien and hostile environment—not our colleagues on the faculty, for they were easy to know, since, like us, most of them were urban imports—but the people in the town and country whose lives were tied to the rural community. Margaret belonged to a circle of ladies, farmers' wives, and became quite popular with them. But we found we had to move on. The image of the straight line told us that. And, every May, in and around the principal's peculiar form of bargaining, I would go down to Berkeley and wrestle with possibilities at teaching agencies. Sometimes we were afraid we would 'never get out'. Like the time I almost thought I had a job in a fine high school near Palo Alto, with a good salary schedule. The reason given for accepting the other man—for it had narrowed down to two of us—was a single grammatical error in my letter of application—a confusion of 'like' for 'as'. It was several weeks before we could laugh about it. We were truly of the depression generation. The significance of getting and holding a job was far out of proportion to what it was with other generations, the sheiks and flappers of the 1920's, the World War II youth, or the post-war period of prosperity.

The accidental nature of events that happened to us strengthened my naturalist convictions, and I was quite prepared to agree with Frank Norris in *The Octopus* that we were victims of blind titanic forces beyond our control in a meaningless and empty universe. One could conquer, one could wrest the pawns from the chessboard of destiny, however, if one had sufficient will, energy, and ambition. Yet the 'break' that came with my employment at a large Junior College seemed like pure coincidence. After a month of interviewing superintendents and principals I had heard vaguely there was an opening. I drove up and walked into the president's office. There were twenty applicants. 'I would like to throw my hat in the ring,' I announced with all the bravo I could summon. And to break a deadlock between three applicants from the local high schools, he had no other choice than that of hiring an 'outside' man. I had come just at the right time. Margaret was in the mountains and I barrelled up the highway in nothing flat to arrive at our camp at midnight. 'I got the job. I got the job,' I remember shouting into the pine forest. We spent most of the night planning.

The mirror dissolves again and fragments of vision emerge from our four years in the new location. Our first house was a little shack out on the hardpan converted swampland west of the college. That winter the rains came in intermittent deluges and we were surrounded by a muddy lake most of January. The car was our row-boat and, when the toilet backed up, for days at a time we had to go to a nearby service station to take care of our necessities.

Then Margaret's father helped us purchase a house. Here was something of our own, a real garden, pleasant rooms, a small foothold on the security that comes with substance and property. John was born in an Oakland hospital and, as in Eric's case, I arrived several hours after the circumstances attending John's birth. Both boys had come in the morning on days when I was teaching!

Another ball of twine followed into the labyrinth, in the hope it would lead us to treasure, was the semester following Pearl Harbour, in which I took a leave to write a book which I called *Bonanza Basin*. I had been gathering notes on the story of irrigation and agriculture in the Great Sacramento-San Joaquin Basin. My idea was to write a kind of biography of an American region, one that had begun with the gold rush, one unique in its agricultural pattern, in which men wrestled with the soil, themselves, and others for the recurrent bonanzas that had evoked such novels as *The Octopus* or Steinbeck's *Grapes of Wrath*. I had been turned down for a navy commission because of my eyes. With a family to support I was not anxious to go in as a private unless drafted and, although the draft board blew hot upon my neck at times, I was never called. Too young for the first war, a bit too old for the second, I thus missed the two great adventures, if one can call them that, that nudged two generations, one just behind, the other just before me.

We moved to a lonely ranch cabin lent to us by a friend. It perched precariously on a bluff 800 feet above the sea south of the Big Sur River. The nearest grocery was in Carmel, fifty miles away, and our supplies came by general delivery every third day. We did not have much money to go on and lived, as much as possible, off the land. For salads and soup, Meg used to go off in the morning, Eric just beginning to walk, John on her back, and pick bags of watercress in a nearby ravine. We wrestled with a crowbar for abalone. A neighbour, a retired editor who was writing a novel and earned his immediate expenses by writing for *True Detective Magazine*, supplied us with fish. He was a creature of strange moods who went on a three-day drunk once a month. At such times he became quite enamoured with Margaret and would come to visit us with his rifle, which he handled very carelessly. We usually managed to get him to sleep and I would bundle him into the car, drive down the road two miles, and lug him into his cabin. A farmer who lived three miles straight up the Santa Lucia range, which rose magnificently right out of the sea, supplied us with deer meat and extras from a large garden of tomatoes, string beans, squash, and potatoes. Game wardens rarely made their appearance—'I would shoot them if they did,' he calmly announced—and since he was in perennial war with game that encroached upon his sparse pasture land, we were rarely without a haunch of venison hanging from the back porch.

I went to the Big Sur for a reason—to write—and, though I failed, the by-products of the experience remain sharply etched in my memory. At night the surf pounded against the cliffs far below and the moon bathed the high and naked Santa Lucia range with white light. We ate out on the porch and the October sunsets emblazoned with molten gold the vast ocean that stretched to infinity before us. The cabin had been hand-made, in the days before a road was put into the region. The doors hung on leather hinges, the crude redwood flooring was unplaned. Only the windows had been imported, and that from a boat that had come as close as it could to the perilous rocks on the coastline, the baggage being transferred to shore by an improvised cable. We read by candlelight and cooked on a wood stove. I had brought along volumes of Robinson Jeffers, for it was this strange poet who had immortalized this country. My naturalism was further confirmed. Spengler's *Decline of the West* had also done its work with me, as with Jeffers. Many of my generation became Marxists. I, rather, became a Spenglerian.

> And why do you cry, my dear, why do you cry?
> It is all in the whirling circles of time.
> If England goes down and Germany up
> The stronger dog will still be on top.
> All in the turning of time.
> If civilization goes down, that
> Would be an event to contemplate.
> It will not be in our time, alas, my dear,
> It will not be in our time.

I was writing in competition for the Knopf prize for the best work in non-fiction on an American region. As I learned later, there were over 800 applicants who sent, as I did, sample chapters and an outline to the publisher. And, as I wrote, I became more and more uneasy. Instead of letting the notes and the story shape itself, listening hard for the material, I kept charging in with vast intuitive plans and counter-plans that kept upsetting my chapter arrangements. Simply put, I bogged down in the morass of notes and a score or two of 'styles'. I was like a drunken sailor who had lost his rudder.

But Margaret hung on and, even now, I do not know what she

31

really thought. Perhaps she had faith that some day one of my enthusiasms would pay off. I would like to think so. And, if it had not been for that ten-day wind the following summer during our High Sierra vacation, we would never have undertaken the final plunge, the attempt to wrest a PH.D. from the University of California in the middle of the war years. Perhaps this fragment of my fairy-tale life with Margaret could all be lumped under the title 'High Wind in the Sierra'. Her cancer would have occurred, anyway, if we had stayed where we were. But the drama of the last stage in the myth—departure, initiation, the road of trials, apotheosis—began with the decision made in a Sierra camp and, symbolically, ended at another high Sierra wilderness region when the incurable disease returned, and, coming with it, the void into which Margaret disappeared.

The first camp, that summer after the book, was six miles from Emerald Bay and up three thousand feet. It nestled under some white granite cliffs, down which tumbled a waterfall from a lake above. Our camp was on a promontory with heather, juniper, and lodge-pole pine, and more granite. The lake curved in on one side; the stream tumbled in on the other. Now the wind is significant only because with the warm August sun bathing the high country, the day was usually crowded with many things to do, hiking, exploring, fishing, 'boating' on a crude raft, swimming in the icy water, and so on. But when a rare Washoe wind sets in to blow not just in the afternoon, as is usual in this country in summer, but all day and all night, the air becomes very cold, particularly from about three in the afternoon to nine or ten the following morning. We had not counted on the rare wind. We did not have enough warm clothing, so we stayed in our sleeping-bags much of the time. The fire blew so much smoke that we could use it only for brief meals. We had not much to do except play tic-tat-toe in the dust in front of our lean-to, read over and over the one book we had brought—and think.

Or rather, *I* thought. I had not secured the Knopf prize, not even an honourable mention. But I had all those damned notes. Now suppose we went to Berkeley, took a leave from the Junior College, and I got a PH.D. in American history. Couldn't I use those notes for my dissertation? And maybe with the war on and changes of personnel I could get into a university or four-year college as a professor. Scratch an English teacher and you will find that when he was young he wanted to write the Great American Novel. Scratch a junior college teacher and you will find someone who believes he just missed out on a university job.

'Why didn't we think of it before,' Margaret cried, her eyes dancing. 'I will get a job. Mummy will be glad to have the boys near her. And in two years. . . .'

'Two years and I'll be assistant professor at Cal—maybe.'

The ball was in again and the big wind did it. We were not to put ourselves out as hostages to fortune. We did not consider all the imponderables. One never does. Given our natures, we had to do what we did. If we had been more conservative, more careful in hoarding the minutiae of existence, our lives would have been quite different. Looking back, it is hard to say where the 'should' or 'ought' is. Something in us drives us to be what we are, to pursue the thread of our individuation.

*   *   *

We found that it was not easy to move from one town to another during the war. We had sold our inland house but there was nary a house for sale, within our means, near the university. Nor even one to rent, particularly if one had children. A boarding house of war-workers, most of them from Arkansas and Oklahoma, the only place that would take us, again because of children, is a good setting for gathering material for a work of fiction, but hardly a place for a family of four. For six months we lived in one room of an old firetrap, our heat gas, with no vent, the meals monotonous slumgullion.

It was during this time that the university teaching hope was dispelled, quite kindly, by a professor. I was too old to start on the low salary of a teaching assistant. A man must get his PH.D. in his twenties, not his thirties, and start at the bottom. Had I published in the Quarterlies? Very well, I resigned myself, I would go on for the PH.D. and go back to the junior college. Meanwhile, Margaret faithfully kept at her job. But we were beginning to lose our hold on the boys, who were in nursery school and who were beginning to react to the boarding house, the uprooting from their first home, and the absence of both parents all day.

The small modest home we finally purchased, at a loss, seemed like a bright treasure. We were again in our own home. A sandbox and a swing in the small back-yard gave us, we felt, our family back again. A fishpond in front and violas and petunias to plant gave my hands a much-needed feeling of roots. I was getting tired of studying German and French, preparing for my writtens, chasing up papers for my seminars, and, in between, teaching spare time as an assistant in journalism and history. Two full fellowships, with no stipulations about teaching, were a great help. And, of course, my wife's father, despite a quarrel that rancored, was of great help financially.

I recall that day in July, 1945, quite vividly. Victory Day, the completion of the war in Europe, was just around the corner. I was mowing the front lawn, a small patch between two avocado trees, when Margaret came home from a visit to the doctor with the announcement that she had some kind of lump in her breast. It could be a benign tumour. Yes, it could be malignant. I confess it was almost the first time I had heard those words, benign, malignant. We were scared. I remember waiting all morning, two days later, while she was in surgery. I remember the noiseless, monstrous clock in the waiting-room of the hospital high on a hilltop in San Francisco. I remember pacing in front of the high window that looked down upon a concrete courtyard, the bright sun spilling through the fog and upon a pot of fading plants. I remember restlessly thumbing the back issues of fading magazines.

It was precisely 12:01 when a nurse tapped me on the shoulder and there Margaret lay, pale, her dark luminous eyes closed, her red mouth white, her body concealed by a white sheet. I shook hands with the great specialist, a tall man with a sombre face. 'Sorry to meet you in circumstances like this. She is all right now. It was a long operation. She's all right now.'

Pacing before that clock all morning had left a kind of bong in my head. I was walking in a dream. How did he mean, 'all right?' But I could see he was trying to evade me, for he suggested I go back and talk to the family doctor. And there, with her, the fat lady doctor with her wry smile and the glasses she kept removing and wiping and putting back comically on the bridge of her nose, I felt easier. Was . . . Margaret . . . all right? I could hear the tyre-screech of a taxi-cab outside and the rumbling noise from the street and I felt safe in the antiseptic calm that the doctor wove, like a spell, in her office.

34

'Sure, give her ten days and you can take her home. Nothing like home for a sick person. She'll hurt for a couple of days. We'll give injections. We're lucky, you know, to have had that surgeon. The old boy was going on vacation yesterday morning.'

'I mean, really all right. It was malignant, wasn't it?'

'Yes. He had to remove a lot. By the way, have you got someone to take care of the children? Someone to come in for the day?'

'The kids are staying in the mountains with her family.'

'Good! Your wife's lucky to have someone like you for a nurse. I understand you are quite a cook, a real home man.'

'Doc, when will she get up?'

'All right, Mr. Pelgrin, all right.'

'Naturally I want to know.'

'All?'

'Naturally.'

'All right. I'm sorry. I have just talked to the surgeon. Your wife has about four years to live. Maybe five. Maybe ten. Who can tell.'

'Or less?'

'You'll have to take that chance, Mr. Pelgrin. Frankly, it could as easily be four months as four years or four weeks. You never know about things like this, I mean from the breast into the lung. Be good to her. Figure out some story to tell her. Keep her encouraged. Keep a stiff upper lip. The whole family depends on you, now.'

I will never forget that afternoon. Margaret was 'under', the nurse assured me, and could not be seen until the next day. I remember the fog breaking over the San Francisco hills and swirling in ribbons of grey cotton around the hospital on the hill. There was a bar down the street and I bought myself two shots of whisky, but the hot stuff seemed to fall away in my mouth, as though it were rusty water. There was even a church, slightly down the hill by one block, and while the service station fellow fixed a spare tyre, I pushed open the large panelled door and stepped inside. The church was a great cavern, empty of people. I stared, in the hollow half-darkness, at the stained glass windows beyond the altar. What I had remembered as a boy was Jesus in a red gown, his hand upraised, the apostles standing about in brittle and dumb silence, the two lambs frolicking and higher up the panoply of angels and clouds and heavenly mists, but what I had remembered was lost to me now. Curiously, this experience of Margaret's operation was far more shaking than *my* encounter!

Then I realized, fully realized, how little, how very little, the angels on those brittle panes of glass had to do with my problem. This great hollow building could suggest but not explain the mystery, and the mystery, I saw for the first time in my life, the mystery that was the plight of all mankind, was unexplainable fantasy. Not angels, fantasy. Not rational science, fantasy. You lived in an upside down situation, and you left it, and there was a crazy time for birth and a crazy time for death and a crazy time for joy and a crazy time for sorrow.

Well, what do you make of it, those words in Ecclesiastes: 'A time for joy, a time for sorrow, a time to be born, and a time to die, a time to plant and a time to pluck up that which is planted.' I cried a bit and for a moment I was one of Homer's heroes. I had always wondered why such brave men as those who fought at Troy burst into tears when they greeted each other when some affliction had come upon them. Small boys don't cry, I was taught. It was hard to cry and it wasn't fashionable. I remembered suddenly the last time I cried—not for Major Fuzzy, but a very distant time, when I was six. We were camping in some deep grove of trees. It must have been mountain country, before I went to Central America. I recalled the ferns that draped along the bank of a small, amber stream, and the great pillars of red-wood trunk that disappeared in the leaf-branched sky. It was gloomy and very, very sad. But it was beautiful, too, the stillness, the indirect light that slanted downward from the concealed sun. I was in tears because the forest was so immense, so overpowering, so uncomprehending, and the experience so beautiful.

So, on that lonely sunlit afternoon, the immense and incomprehensible facts of life and love and death and time pushed Mark and Margaret into an ever-more urgent seeking after meaning. Two years after the operation, they went together to a seminar on the teachings of Jesus, while prior to that they had, as Mark said, 'discovered' Dr. Fritz Kunkel. That is, they had begun reading his books, and had started working on some of his suggestions about self-

36

knowledge and religious meanings. Margaret was deeply affected by both of these experiences, and the insight thus obtained, plus her work in personal Jungian analysis, supported her spirit during her last few years. As has been already said, for Mark these new influences were crucial, and helped him to see the 'purposes of God' as he walked with Margaret, to the best of his ability, into her darkness, and as he had also to walk into his own later valley. He wrote in his journal during this time: 'My spiritual problem was now clear. The second half of my life . . . was to be a journey in discovery of personal meaning. . . . I yearned for a compass, a direction, and was increasingly aware of my need for reverence, for awe in the face of the eternal mystery, for genuine humility.' These things Mark and Margaret gave themselves to in the intervening years, while the life of home, family, and work went on its usual way.

SKETCH WRITTEN IN 1955

Four years after Margaret's operation, we took another pack trip, this time with the children, for they were six and nine, just barely old enough to make it. It was two days into Hamilton Lakes from where we parked our car at headquarters in Sequoia National Park. Then we followed a winding upward trail to Skyparlour Meadow and Moraine Lake. From this high plateau, with the curious name of Chagoopa, the Whitney range towered to the east, the Kaweahs to the west; and the Great Divide, with Red Peak, to the north. A steep drop brought us into the abyss of the Kern and in three more days we were on our way up the marbled granite ridge to a finger of lakes nestled under a peak that faced the south. Here we camped at almost the last timberline tree, a gnarled old juniper, bent and broken in the wind. We were back in the high country. This time there was no wind. Despite the elevation of 12,400 feet, the weather was almost hot. It is hard to say what brings people to these massifs and bleak cirques, these treeless bottomless lakes, these stark granite cliffs. To the uninitiated, the high country is no place for man creatures. To the initiated, there is a kind of beyondness in the bleak cliffs and the tiny dappled meadows, lush with bluebells, Indian Paint Brush, the dozens of varied hues that speckle the greensward that slopes to the tumbling brooks.

One day in camp at Wright's Lake, Margaret developed a

cough, with a kind of wheezing sound, as though there were water in her lungs. We did not tell ourselves, then, that it was the return of The Lump. But we clambered back to civilization, over Forester's Pass, down Bub's Creek to the King's and the pack station as fast as we could. We clung to the hope, of course, that it was pneumonia. But we knew. The memory of the rocks remained, too, along with the bright green life of the meadows and the green heart of the California August that is the high country, and the dancing person that was one part of Margaret. Perhaps there is a kinship between the white granite of the Velma Lakes or the white granite that loomed above Wright's Lake and the flaming words of Isaac Pennington, the seventeenth century English Quaker:

Know the light, the eternal light of life, the little glimmerings and shinings of it in thy soul. This comes from the rock, to lead thee to the rock; and if thou follow it, it will fix thee upon the rock where thou canst not be shaken.

These words we could quote easily and understandably at Wright's Lake. At Velma Lake they would have been incomprehensible. What happened in between, those four years, was the search for the thimble in the well.

The death of his wife was the beginning of a period of upheaval, suffering, and confusion for Mark. There were the children to be cared for. His job was demanding. Debts had piled up during his wife's long illness. All these things he tried to handle, not always either smoothly or successfully.

Then during the summer following his wife's death, Mark returned to the seminar on the teachings of Jesus, seeking ever more deeply for a religious meaning to what had happened. He was decisively affected by the challenge of the great paradox of Jesus, 'Whosoever shall seek to gain his life shall lose it; but whosoever shall lose his life shall preserve it.' (Lk. 17: 33.) This meant, for Mark, the difference between protecting himself from life by artificial barriers and escapes, and letting go of his defences that he might find himself. He did not see it as referring to physical life and death, nor was he now or later concerned with a life beyond what he knew as life. But from here on, Mark's religious growth was central to him, through all the bumblings and vicissitudes which were part of his progress.

38

His meeting of Ruth and his marriage to her marked a new turn of the path. The demands of the world increased as responsibilities mounted—but genuine joy was not lacking. Little time was available for journals or other writings, so that Mark did not leave much 'autobiographical' material on this period. He did take time, however, to attend further seminars. A few excerpts from letters, and a short journal entry, give a general picture of him.

EXCERPTS, FROM LETTERS TO HIS SECOND WIFE, ABOUT SEMINARS

We started our seminar yesterday morning with the Mary and Martha episode in the Synoptic Gospels, in which Martha chides Mary in front of Jesus for not helping with the housework, since Martha has more than she can do and must bustle around to serve everyone. The point is that Jesus chides Martha and not Mary. Jesus says to Martha, 'Be not anxious'. From there we moved to the problem that anxiety accompanies the making of choices and one must make choices to become free (i.e., conscious—away from collectivism to the discovery of one's self), so anxiety inevitably accompanies individuation. However, the Way is to learn about different kinds of anxiety and to be able to confront the problem. Two quotes from Kierkegaard were appropriate here: his stress that openness to possibility is affirmation of oneself (i.e., that one must be willing to face openness and change, hence choice and anxiety). 'We confront the problem of freedom when we confront the ALARMING possibility of being able.' And to what extent was the original construction of The Lord's Prayer—'Lead us into temptation but be sure we make the right choices'? This brought us to an interesting discussion of Satan as the other side of God. Satan in the Old Testament plays a positive role. He is the one who throws before the conservative individual the possibility of new choices. He is, in short, the tempter in the fullest sense. One could almost say he is God's active side. Or, to put it another way, where would we have been if he had NOT tempted Adam and Eve out of the Garden of Eden and onto the thorny road to human consciousness? But the task is too great!

These seminars have been going for ten years. This is the eleventh. Coming back again makes me realize that they offer (or rather the ideas developed by the leaders offer) something much more real and positive for an approach to living today than any religious institution or any mechanistic approach. And the thing that amazes me is that it is so close to what some of our poets—like T. S. Eliot—are saying. Also the quotations we have had from Kierkegaard are tremendous.

Today we discuss the problem of egocentricity and anxiety. The passage read after breakfast was beautifully written—I will see if I can send it along. It has to do with living in today rather than in tomorrow but not today alone but today in cooperation with eternity which is greater than living for tomorrow or today. Meaning, of course, get as much out of today in terms of meaning as possible.

Tonight we are spending the evening singing Bach Chorales, which the group assures me is not a hard thing to do. . . . As long as a strong, practised and sure voice is behind me, I can sing all right. I just wobble terribly when I am left on my own to read a line of music!

I wish you were here.

Love,
Mark.

We sang Bach Chorales last night—and to my great surprise, it worked. The group was divided into four parts—I sang bass. After several rehearsals on each part, we put it together and it was surprising! Of course, in each group there was at least one singer who could read music easily and had had glee club or chorale experience.

I cannot resist copying a passage from Kierkegaard because of its analogy with something we have discussed in acting and because it is so moving:

The most important thing in life is to be in the correct position, to assume the correct position. It is well known that in front of the actor, blinded as he is by the footlights, there is the deepest darkness, the blackest night. One might think that this would discompose him, render him uneasy. But no, ask him, and thou shalt hear him admit that this is precisely what gives him support, makes him calm, keeps him in the enchantment of deception. On the other hand, it would discompose him if he could see any single individual, catch a glimpse of an auditor. So it is with the next day. One sometimes complains and finds it tragic that

40

the future is so dark before one. Ah, the misfortune is just this, that it is not dark enough when fear and presentment and expectation and earthly impatience glimpse the next day! One who rows his boat turns his back to the goal towards which he is labouring. So it is with the next day. When by the help of eternity a man lives absorbed in today, the more decisively does he turn his back upon the next day, so that he does not see it at all. If he turns around, eternity is confused before his eyes, it becomes the next day. But if for the sake of labouring more effectively towards the goal (eternity) he turns his back, he does not see the next day at all, whereas by the help of eternity he sees quite clearly today and its task.

Which, put another way, boils down to, 'If, in time, one had only this day to live, what would one make of it?'

Yesterday we discussed egocentricity and anxiety and some very interesting things were said about the relation of anxiety to children—when it begins, etc. Out of it there developed, as most important, the idea that ego-structure is the opposite of egocentricity. Not enough people have genuine ego-structure—pride in themselves in the real sense. It would seem to me that your creativity in the arts—and you have plenty of it—by this token is one of your salvations. It is honest, real, creative, not illusory—and certainly in no way egocentric as far as I can see. Corollary to this: you ought to do as much of it as you can; not restrict it; unless you can find other well-springs of creativity, as in the widget!

Yesterday's seminar was very interesting, touching on social pressure and anxiety. Both of the leaders stressed that, for the analyst, one of the biggest problems is the patient's anxiety over social prestige, keeping up with the Joneses, and competition with others. We all agreed that competition was neurosis-breeding, and that the real competition is when one competes with himself rather than with another.

There are some extremely wise and mature older people in this group whom I would like to get to know but they always seem to be reading or something out of the seminar.

Love,
Mark.

Probably because all of this group has been to the seminars a number of times, this is a fascinating experience. The group contributions are so good and so full of insight that there is very little

I feel like chipping in with. I just like to listen. Some of the older people have really worked out some bases for living rich lives that I am only just beginning to see. I am more and more impressed with the extraordinary soundness, the genuine relatedness possible with the Jungian approach to our human nature.

We are using the central experiences of Jesus—the baptism and wilderness—as a taking-off point for a theme which we find throughout the Records—the primary action of Jesus in the role of Choice, Personal Responsibility, and the meaning of sacrifice. Yesterday we discussed the nature of the Deity, masculine and feminine components, etc.—in short, the symbols of the archetypes of God. Today we discuss the meaning of Sonship, meaning of the Self, Religious experience and relationship. I am taking careful notes to share with you.

Love,
Mark.

Yesterday's seminar was most fascinating . . . especially when we began to see the way in which each of us plays a tiny role, or a larger one (as did Jesus), in furthering and helping create the incompletion that is God. Today the session involved what, in us, hinders completion or fulfilment of ourselves and therefore the Spirit.

There are some magnificent art books here—and I am right now especially fascinated by the delightful, abundant, rich gardens in the Persian Miniatures.

Last night we did moving to music—which was quite exciting. We simply danced by ourselves (no one is supposed to look at anyone else) to some Bach, Appalachian Spring, some jazz, some primitive music, some Ravel, etc.

Love,
Mark.

EXCERPT FROM JOURNAL, FALL, 1954

For the past year, and particularly these past few months, I have had a probably deceptive sense of being 'mature and objective', as though participating in the world with greater efficiency and understanding than I ever had before. It is true that I am teach-

ing more effectively—doing things now in a short time that used
to take me a long time. I 'see through' things better now, I think,
and can cut through what used to take many words with a class,
to simple statements. The students seem to like my teaching a
good deal. At home Eric is becoming very enjoyable to talk with.
John still presents the problem with Ruth.

Often Ruth and I seem to have little to talk about and I read in
bed and she goes to sleep. This bothers me. But I get so tired
teaching during the day. The problem is distinguishing 'real
maturity' and 'objectivity' and efficiency, from the fact that I
sometimes feel 'dry' 'in a dry month' and probably lack feeling
relationship. It is a real struggle to get 'this other one', and sometimes my mind slips back into a 'fairy tale' mood, but life
suddenly intervenes with its terrific schedule demands—getting
that set of papers corrected, preparing for that course, worry
about that story I must have for the Sunday night story club,
etc.

HIS REVISION OF A FAMOUS PRAYER, 1954

> O, Lord, give us the strength
> To do the difficult.
> Give us the courage to
> Abandon the Impossible. And
> Give us the Judgement to
> Distinguish between them.

*Less than a year after this last journal entry, Mark became ill,
which illness proved to be the precursor to his death, and which illness also he himself so eloquently talked about in ' The Encounter'.
But it must not be assumed that all the interim years were grave and
grey. Much of delight and laughter, of love, of work enjoyed, was
contained in those years.*

*Twins were born, adding noise and vitality, and more involve-
ment, to the entire household. Trips into the high mountain country
were taken, including the entire family. As the two older children
grew into adolescence, certain problems grew, also, inevitably,
because Mark had had to play too many roles for them during their
mother's illness and after her death, and thus they could not know
precisely who he was. So life was up and down, drawing many rich
opposites into itself.*

Mark gave much thought now to teaching as a profession to which he knew he could give. His creative contributions were many and real, from his revisions of teaching methods and programmes, to his gentle but enthusiastic relationships to his students—and he began to look forward to a future of true satisfaction in his profession. But his days were so full, his family so demandingly enjoyable, such leisure as was available so vibrant with things to do, that Mark had little time to record himself in a journal or elsewhere.

Then, with five years of this new sort of life behind him and presumably an eternity of years ahead, he was told that 'possibly' he had cancer. The midpoint of life had been reached for Mark Pelgrin —at least as he saw it. It was not a chronological but a psychological dividing line. All the speculations and the insights of the past, oriented toward an indefinitely prolonged future, had now to be made manifest, if possible, in a fore-shortened Now. Time was no longer something to be hoped about—it had to be used!

Ruth and Mark went together to a seminar at the end of that summer of Mark's temporary convalescence. Mark returned to Jungian analysis and worked devotedly at his 'journey toward self'; the section of this book called 'The Inward View' deals specifically with this phase of his life. Mark had about eight months left him—although he did not know that—in which to fulfil his days. He did the very best he could with them until spring came, and with it his second illness and operation, and his death. The following pages are Mark's own struggles to set forth some of the major life events of the period beginning with his first operation.

SEVEN JOURNAL EXCERPTS, 1955

And so I returned, dark in mood, from white-sheeted anaesthetic silence of the hospital to the busy little world that is our home. The walls were there and the roof solidly in place as it has always been. The stairs led to the basement or to the children's room. The garden was as beautiful as ever. The redwood tree stood passive against the wind from the coast (now for the first time, and the blear-eyed side of it), the hydrangeas blooming pink and white as they had before I went to the hospital (but a flaw in the perfection) and the boys busy with plans, and Ruth tending a thousand and one details that make up the life of that complex person, a modern housewife.

But the steel track of time had slipped for me and I skidded along it with uncertain direction, lingering now upon a future imagined event that seemed close to what the doctor said was probably inevitable, now to a past experience that suddenly became more vivid than the immediate present, now to a dream that became more real that what had seemed to be 'reality'. The world I knew, the confines of the known, had suddenly been cracked by an explosion from the *mysterium tremendum*.

The first week home I dreamed of a black coffin with a white rose upon it. A tall man with dark eyes hovered there, with a red rose between his teeth. The rose became a fire at the end of a long corridor. Shadow figures moved up and down near the fire, endlessly circling in a solemn ritual. 'In my end is my beginning', they were saying. I plunged down the corridor to join them but they suddenly disappeared, and I awoke to find the morning sun streaming through the windows.

In the kitchen beyond, the kettle was humming merrily and the familiar routine of morning brought me to this tender and commonplace moment in time.

*　　　*　　　*

And so the summer passes, the incision heals, the vital currents flow again, although I am tired more quickly than I used to be and I try to slow down what were formerly my fast jerky movements; I am to all intents and purposes well. Well in health except for the knot, the insoluble puzzling knot I carry inside, as though the man at the gate of the year, that strange shadowy fellow who broods over our lives, had decided to bring his vulture self down and fly inside me. 'God's idiot brother,' I say to myself ironically. I will come to know him better and I will ask him, why? Who am I, anyway? What, if anything, can I do about it? What about the younger children? Is it fair to turn them fatherless into the woods, the labyrinth of life? Is it not possible for You to arrange another time, another place for our final encounter? They are very small. Do you expect to achieve greater glory or power by depriving them of one who can at least shelter their stumbling efforts to grow, to become human, until they can stand on their own feet? In my mind's eye I can see them walking in a forest of giant redwoods hand in hand like mythological characters with a giant peering from behind the elderberry bushes or leering from the great branches that interlock above their heads. I am frightened for them, for they are lost, terribly lost, and my heart turns over with a thump and a single word comes to my lips, why, why! . . .

*   *   *

And he has come home from the hospital, this fellow, this blue-eyed school teacher, this bundle of ambitions, contradictions and complex experiences, and he finds that the game of life he has played and for which he had always called the signals has become a rout! The signals instead are called by a tiny mass of twisted cells, inflamed, unpredictable, at work in the caverns of his body, and I become he—for I sometimes feel I am hovering there in the ceiling of my room looking down on this other guy in the bed and upon the books on the desk and the lampstand. I am a stranger to myself, a stranger here, myself, and there are two of us. The one, lying or getting up or taking off his shoes, and the one watching, intently watching. 'What now, little man, what now, fellow,' I ask of him.

*   *   *

The summer walks fast and July becomes August, the body restores and heals. I watch while with delight this fellow shuffles into his old clothes, takes the clippers and prunes the garden hedge or, extraction of the moment, he makes a romp with the children, or a piece of old crayon on paper, or the getting of a meal, or the reading of a book, or when the feelings change, the despair when he is suddenly confronted with the future. And I feel like saying to him, 'All right, fellow, you have had a strange life, all mortals have strange lives and I feel with you and this I'll admit is the strangest experience of all. Now what meaning do you make of it? Can you find the why in it?' And I weep for him and he weeps for me and we weep together. Jesus wept, we can weep, can't we? And then it comes to him that he is a hero in a myth—for are we not all heroes, in one way or another, and are not our lives myths, fairy tales, legends that we have created? He is Theseus about to wander in the labyrinth in search of the minotaur that must be slain. But where is Ariadne with the golden thread who will help him discover a passage in the tortuous corridors and wells that lead to the monster? And what is the monster? The doctors have pronounced their verdict, the monster is within, it is irrevocable, there it lies waiting against the passage of a near future time. Old Thuggee himself with the strangling noose—or is this really the monster? The doctors had named the monster, but did this mean the verdict was final?

Well, and so I argue and reason with him and we wander about the garden together. He takes up the hose and turns on the faucet and the water sprinkles the patch of marigolds by the fence and we talk as man to man—he, encased in the body, and I the spirit, the self, the unseen presence within. I of the dancing, the rose, and the fire, and he the clumsy one, the stranger, the hero in the myth we have to complete for each other. For we are one, but we are two and what belongs to him belongs to me and what I am he is, and what he is I am, and the end is in the beginning.

In this endlessly circling dance of life I say to him: 'Why must the monster be "science says", or "the moving finger of time writes"? Cannot what is behind time write the moving finger?'

He replies: 'Have you considered all the possibilities? Perhaps it is the irrational, non-scientific side that will save you if you really want to be a hero, and if you are indeed a hero in a modern myth. Then you must first realize that the steps in the way are never really known in advance, and that the monster will be slain and the treasure found in the labyrinth of time precisely by way of the irrational, the ambiguous. Surprise and the willingness to be surprised is of the essence in the hero's success. That is the meaning of creative intelligence, that you are not committed to any fixed preview of the future. Accept what is, with complete openness. Have you really considered all the possibilities? Lie closer to yourself, to me, to the dreams, for I am an honest fellow though my way seems strange to you. You are called to adventure. You could, of course, refuse the call. You wish to invoke God, supernatural aids, you must cross the threshold, you must go into the belly of the whale for, like Jonah, the whale is within and you must let him swallow you for a time.'

'But my cancer? The doctor was quite clear in what he said.'

'Ah, but note that you say "my cancer", as though you lovingly possessed it. Immediately that you say "my cancer" it possesses you. Check yourself when your attitude is not open, completely open, as to outcome. "This thing has happened to me." . . . "my cancer", are sentences your lips form but in themselves will prevent you from crossing the threshold. They will close off your opportunities to listen to what life says and you will lose your way in the labyrinth. This is the supreme experience in your life, a crisis for you of dramatic proportions. If you are really to be a hero, walk unafraid into the darkness. The man at the gate of the year will be there when you do and take your hand and lead you safely into the unknown.'

'I must say that I am impressed. Naturally I will try anything. Any of the regular things people are supposed to do in circumstances like this. Are you trying to say that if I just try to think myself well I will be well?'

'More obstacles to your journey, as you must clearly see. The path for you must be wholly untried. It is the path of what is truly you, what is really you. We don't know the outcome nor can we find an orthodox ritual. "Science says," or "I'll take this cup," are your orthodox methods—they haven't worked too well, have they? For you it has to be the path of the wholly new, the wholly untried commitment to the paradoxical, irrational side of the universe. This has always been the hero's way. And do not expect that the skies will open and the earth will be rent asunder for you. Why does evil rage when God is silent? Because we expect what will happen in terms of big and noisy signs. Remember how in the great myths it is the little thing, the crazy donkey with bedraggled hair, not the handsome stallion, that carries the hero to the sleeping princess. It is the little feather that speaks.'

'And will I not bungle this journey, too, as I have all the others? Muddling Mark, that is what I was called when I was a child. As I look back now, all of what I have done seems so stumbling, so inarticulate, so awkward. I am a graceless, unleavened lump of mammalian substance. I am. . . .'

'Precisely. And how else would the spirit work in matter but clumsily? To move over into the shadow you will have to be Mary, not Martha. To sit and listen at the feet of your universe as though you were listening for the first time. You see, my dear Mr. Pelgrin, whether you like it or not you are in process of transformation; all that you have been must be held in suspension so that you can let me work. What is instinctually and really you, you have to learn to be at home with. It will be much like learning a new skill, like driving a strange car with all the gears reversed.'

'And where do we start this crazy and strange process?'

'Like the alchemist of old, you are the clay that must be transformed. Let the spirit work in that clumsy material.'

* * *

48

Yesterday my cup nearly ran over! Strange that since I am given a year or two I should have enjoyed a day with such happiness and content. It is as though everything stood out for itself, every little thing, sharply defined, timeless, to be enjoyed in and for itself. The babies were fun to feed at lunch. Susan is busy naming things, finding words. Lynn listens to her, watches me, and giggles. They will sit for an hour in their high chairs in the kitchen watching me make soup, or get lunch. Ruth, bless her, was in our room, finishing up the painting and the pieces. John and I worked in the herb garden, getting it ready, and we played ping-pong in the evening. His wall occasionally breaks and he is subject to swift changes of mood. He seemed quite happy to have Eric home. Eric phoned about five-thirty from the station, back from the pack trip. He certainly has the light touch. We picked up his girl and had a fine Italian dinner. Later in the evening we had chocolate. It was so much fun to listen to each one.

Many of the problems that have bothered me, the drinking of wine, the pressing feeling that I am too busy to enjoy this moment of time, the failure to listen, seem to be on the way to solution. It may be, cross fingers, that my brief release, the shortening of my tenure, turns my image or picture around so that the part of me that is obsessed by time changes to a part, as yet crudely developed, that enjoys passage in time. The mysterious role that time plays in our lives!

*　　　*　　　*

I had quite an alarm Sunday night and Monday morning. I have had a lump in my thigh for three weeks. At first I assumed it might be one of the usual sebaceous glands kicking up again— a hangover that I have suffered since my adolescent years, as I once had acne very severely. Well, this lump got larger Sunday, and Sunday night Ruth saw it and asked me what it was. I turned to her savagely and said, 'The cancer returned, of course.' Then I apologized, and said I was really talking to the man upstairs, and I didn't mean her. We were both upset. I said there was no use going to the doctor as obviously it was cancer returned, and I did not want to know about it—to hell with it.

I went to bed and to sleep praying: 'Our Father'—only I had to say 'Father-Father-Father' and 'Mother-Mother-Mother,' like that little boy in Menotti's opera.

So next morning, Jack picked me up, and I started to cry and

49

told him my fears. 'For Christ's sake, go to the doctor right away,' he said. 'You want to know, don't you?' School this day, but it was a strange one, and I went to the doctor and found it was only a sebaceous cyst which he lanced. (But as I had waited in his office I had calculated my chances. About seventy-five per cent cancer, I reasoned. I must have a compulsion to think the worst.)

Jack brought some ale home. Ruth, who had been worried sick all day, and had planned to go to the doctor for me, was overjoyed. Then I puzzled over this. Well now, I said, what is this? I suddenly realized that my life was like being in a play, or seeing a play, and that there were many curtains disclosing many new sets. The curtains were manipulated by opposites and because I had dared to question, to probe, to strive for the kingdom, I had, seemingly, more varied and more strange experiences than I could have anticipated. Something in me impelled curtain after curtain to unroll, but always it was done by these contradictions, pairs of opposites, one on each side of a drawn curtain joined at the middle. This impelling had pushed me into a stage set beyond the superficial. And I suddenly recalled early in youth asking about the beyond, beyond the beyond. But then it was outward, and now I had a deep sense that it was in me. Strangely, I had opened a magazine in the doctor's office, and the page held a 'quality ad' which had a picture of a tree inside a man, and words from Francis Bacon's *Novum Organum*—something about the image in our mind which is privileged to see the *mean and the beautiful*. The universe then is contained in me as it is in each of us, and with our tiny microcosms we are privileged to glimpse for a time the mean and the beautiful, and to strive to fuse these opposites into the unity that is required of every truly mature and spiritual person. For out of the One comes the many, and Many come in pairs—Male and Female, Sky and Earth, and this process of discrimination seems to be the evolving nature of the universe and in a vast drama of interaction with God's handiwork—God himself unfolding into macrocosm-microcosm, world without end in a magnificent circle.

* * *

By way of contrast to the last weekend with its alarm on Sunday night, this week-end was bathed in golden sunshine. We have had an unusually brilliant fall, northern California at its best.

Day after day of autumnal sunshine, with no fog, no wind, the garden seemingly resting in an October stillness that is broken only by a distant truck on the highway, the soft city sounds from the houses below on the flat, the call of a bird in the oak trees or in the pines. The garden, of course, is decked out in its end of the dry season fineness—the geraniums and the fuschias blooming, and ever the fir trees themselves, the redwood, the pines, erect and proud in their symmetry.

My own mood was one of peace and content. The illness and its threat seemed to have enhanced my capacity to quietly be and enjoy,.and I felt genuinely mellow. Saturday night, Ruth and I went to a formal dance and enjoyed it thoroughly. Sunday a.m., too, I abstained from all school work and mostly worked in the garden. Sunday night I just lay around and quietly read—not even that—worked a little on my desk fixing it and talked to Eric a bit, and looked up in Josephus a passage on the Essenes.

One conflict came up, when I failed to go to church. We were broke and didn't even have a dollar, etc., etc. But mainly, I was not sure to what extent the church service really would answer my deep inward need. I was confused as to whether to tell the minister about my problem and to ask for prayer. I felt bothered that I did not carry on with the Adult Sunday School class this fall, though I think it is better if I rest instead. And so on. Perhaps I should have tried to get to the communion service and to feel into the symbolism as it directly relates to me. (I pray daily by myself in a crude sort of way. Indeed, a man in my position becomes a kind of walking prayer.) And was I doing all I could? (Certainly I feel I am, with my analysis and dreams. I sometimes even feel like a walking dream).

When I came home from the hospital I realized I had a big job to do to find meaning in this strange life of mine and this that has suddenly come, to work at the task of some kind of completion of myself, to find fruitful relationships with those around me, and to learn how to be. Now in the business of 'being' there is a middle point between over-conscious purpose and its attendant anxiety, and a lazy desuetude. It is letting things happen. I find a much greater ease, maturity, and skill in teaching a class, in doing many things I used to do badly when I pressed too hard. I do find a kind of new maturity and grace in my approach to things.

51

Yet am I doing all I can? I sometimes try the trick of feeling all the way through me, rather than in my head, and find this helps a good deal to realize that my life, spirit, soul, psyche, is contained in a body which is not an enemy but a friend. I become conscious, of course, when I do this, of 'rumblings' in my stomach, tiny pains in my side, and can see how some people can develop hypochondria. I become tired more than I used to and quite easily, and find it is an enjoyable luxury just to lie down. This way I am more conscious of moods and feelings than I have been before.

At the New Year, 1956, the bells rang in the last five months of Mark Pelgrin's life, although no one could foresee this. He himself only sensed, from an inarticulate and interior wisdom, that time had lost its familiar dimensions, that the 'contradictory armies of the night' were marching towards a final settlement. New Year's Day, together with the few days surrounding it, was spent by Mark and his wife in the company of some of their closest friends from their shared seminar experiences. This all-too-short period in the mountains somehow gave him a renewed awareness of the worth of immediacy. On New Year's Eve, Mark had a last joyful fling at his 'jazz piano'; and as the Old Year breathed away with the last candle flame extinguished, those of us who sat quietly in the firelight of the shadowed living room were merged in the meaning of sacrifice—although most did not yet know the true 'facts'.

Mid-January to mid-March was a period without many journal entries and a only a few poems, as if Mark Pelgrin were 'catching his spiritual breath' for the terminal climb. He continued in analysis, kept up with his teaching and his personal and family life, although his fatigue increased. It still was not clear, however, that cancer was the cause of his physical feelings. He had been giving of his utmost to understand himself, to reach new levels of relationship with his sons—and such intense psychological output is exceedingly tiring. Moreover, as Mark says, even the surgeon wondered whether the gastro-intestinal symptoms could be psychologically triggered. So the ambiguity and the paradox remained in the front of his consciousness.

In early April, with startling suddenness, an acute infection, accompanied by high temperature, sent Mark to the hospital. Medication reduced the infection and the fever, but the jaundice and the itch returned. He was able to go home for a while, to be in his room where, from his bed, he could see his loved redwood tree and his garden beginning to breathe of spring. These were days of rising and falling hopes, of time bearing too great a weight, of practical anxieties, of little girls and dogs romping through his room for delight of life, of physical misery underlining his endless nights. And, as always, he 'wrestled with the angel' for redemption.

The surgeon decided on another operation, so at the end of April he re-entered the hospital. In a six-hour-long operation the surgeon tried everything he knew to alter the condition, but could not. One week later, Mark Pelgrin died.

During the final days, of course, he could not write or paint. He could only be—with such inscrutable thoughts as no other could share. He talked some about the necessary future of his family. He wanted to hear read aloud his favourite passages from T. S. Eliot's 'Four Quartettes'. And he listened to the 'heartbeat of life,' in himself and in the fading world of substance and time. A reproduction of an ancient Chinese cave painting, brought to him by one of his dearest friends, hung on his wall during this week. This he lived with deeply, finding in its balanced beauty a sense of the mystery of the seasons of God, which he had confronted so courageously and for so long.

JOURNAL, JANUARY, 1956

Yesterday, January 3, on the long ten-hour stretch from Southern California home, I was overcome by an extreme desolation of spirit, as though descending to a place in myself where no sun shines, no wind blows, where the seeds lie fallow in the barren sandy soil, where grim black rocks lurk in the shadows, a place in myself of no return. There will be other times like this. So I am setting down the experience exactly as it happened in order that I can perhaps retain some tiny scrap of meaning out of the exhaustion.

We were returning from the New Year's weekend. We had held the last seminar to be held in the large lovely old room with the big fireplace and the intricate rafters, for the seminars are moving to a new place in Northern California. The weekend itself was a bundle of opposites. There were moments of deep-moving humanity, when, for example, in the ritual we evolved out of the group to meet the New Year, we linked hands in the darkness and remained silent while the old fire was taken out of the fireplace and put outside the house and the new fire was lit. There were moments of despair, too, for I was tired all of the time, as I had been much of Christmas vacation. Everyone seemed so full of vitality, except me.

So yesterday morning we left in the Mead's car, Hal driving, Joan in the front seat, Ruth in back, reading, and I cushioned by blankets, my head on my coat, sleeping fitfully. I felt literally exhausted, drained of energy. The darkness within, which enclosed, enveloped me, seemed a strange contrast to the bright, clear, cold day, for the steep and queer California landscape was bathed in liquid sunshine. But there was no wind out there, beyond myself, either, and the dry leaves of the oaks were limp and lifeless on the cold ground.

My mood and the crispness of the sun brought back that bronze feeling about sunlight that I had learned to associate with Margaret and those frightful months immediately after the discovery of her cancer. The sun, I discovered that August and September of 1945, is veiled by demonic powers that bring death as well as life. Fear and terror lurk in the broad open sunlight. In these moments I feel a redness in the bright light, which I call 'bronze,' because it seems so indifferent, so cruel, so lacking in response to human beings and human needs. This bronze feeling makes my knees tremble and I fear new horrors around every corner as though a bronze eye were following me, an evil eye bent on my destruction. I once confided this 'fear and trembling' to an acquaintance, but I could see by his response that we had little communication on the subject. He had not only never felt it but regarded such feelings as weaknesses. Perhaps the John Does of the world are lucky, or perhaps they have missed the left side of the pairs of opposites that are part of the human experience. Perhaps I could say to them, with Laotze,

> The average man is so crisp and so confident
> That I ought to be miserable
> Going on and on like the sea
> Drifting nowhere
> All these people are making their mark in the world,
> While I, pig-headed, awkward,
> Different from the rest,
> Am only a glorious infant still nursing at the breast.

Perhaps I should have said that, then, yesterday, as we began the long climb from the orange groves to the desert that is the freeway up Cajon Pass, but I could not. I was sick at heart and there was no glorious infant in me to be found. Rather, in my troubled imagination, as the white sandstone slid past the car window, I kept saying, 'I must last until February 4 or just past it, for that was Margaret's death date,' or, 'I must last until summer at least because the family needs the money I earn.' The words became a kind of incantation, the word 'last' seeming to settle heavily on every rock and hill that flashed by. And then I reflected on this strange experience of mine, this strange creature, I, always so isolated from the known and sure way, only rarely 'crisp and confident'. Could it be that my analysis, my seminar experiences, have raised demonic powers that would otherwise have slept if I had left them alone? What would it be like to be completely contained in collective religious beliefs and to accept uncritically and with faith such words as those of Father Hall, when I told him about my illness: 'If this is the last year of your life, how beautiful it must be, knowing you will go to your eternal reward.' I felt it was a cheesy remark, one spoken more out of principle and doctrine than out of love and experience, and it revolted me. How nice, how nice if I were only on the light side of the collective unconscious and did not have to worry about differentiation, integrity of myself and what I really think and feel, honest probing into what is really unique and real for me!

It could not be that way. My *karma* has destined me to honesty and integrity of spirit. I must believe what I believe. From a thoughtless intellectual of years ago I have been forced by pain and sorrow into a deep understanding of my unity with the cosmos, a kind of pantheistic unity sometimes. But even that comfort was gone this day, January 2, 1956, and here I was now, shooting along the highway in the Mojave Desert, the Joshua trees blinking at me with their semaphore arms, lifeless like the desert.

Then I made up a list, a memorandum to myself of that which I was prepared to sacrifice as the Old Year wheeled into the New. It was not as easy as the New Year's resolutions I used to make, about not talking so much, or quitting smoking, or resolving to pay more attention to details, etc. When one comes to the prospect of one's own life being sacrificed, resolutions for the future fade away. The question becomes one of omissions and commissions. The only visible signature I will leave in the universe is that upon my children and those who know me. I am sharply aware that I am leaving as much bad as good, as many omissions as commissions, but then this is part of universal human experience, and the sins of the fathers shall live to the second and third generation.

'Well, here I am,' I said to myself, 'I have always been a mountain-top jumper, an intuitive. I have had grandiose visions that have escaped more pedestrian people and, for good and ill, I will these traits to my children. Perhaps they can learn what I learned late, that vision must go hand in hand with experience, that it must be tested by reality, that it must be rooted in the earth and not always up in the clouds. I am willing to sacrifice my verbalism, to resolve to be chaste, in the sense of thinking and feeling only what is closely related to what I am. Sometimes my ideas, like silly geese, have honked me astray. In the little time left I shall not have preconceived ideas. I shall bend, like a reed, to the winds of the universe.'

But the trouble was, in my desolation, that there was no wind and I was no reed, and though I tried hard, I could not feel into the 'glorious infant still nursing at the breast'. Only one thing loomed. That I was sick, that I was going to die, and that I could make no meaning out of the experience.

The Joshua trees kept wagging their semaphore arms in the thin desert air as we approached Lancaster, where man has but a precarious hold of water and stone and board in the vast empty realm of sagebrush—and I cried, silently, for I did not want others in the car to know of my wandering in this wilderness of spirit. I have been afraid of crying, in the past, and have not allowed myself to feel instinctually, directly, as a man should. Crying is not a sissy act. It is a manly act, a recognition of what is deeply masculine in oneself. Too often I have not cried when I should have cried, or not laughed when I should have laughed. Too often the crying and laughing came afterward, like a weak echo 'at' rather than 'with'. I was much impressed by Elizabeth's crying over the death of her nephew, and quite prepared to sacrifice the cautious reserve that had prevented me from re-acting humanly, with feeling, to immediate situations in life.

There is no need to talk more about my list. It all came to the same thing—the need for direct human feeling, humanity as an answer to the depersonalization of our times, love, in short, love. This feeling came for a moment, like a fragment of a spring thaw blowing over the top of the icecap. I had come this far, then. I had at last sensed the deep centre of our humankind. It lies in love, but love that is direct and spontaneous and outgoing, and love that breaks down walls and thaws the chill of the mask, and love that blends the ego and the self, love not as a sentimental greeting card but as a point of tension, a unity of opposites in which dislike attracts like and like attracts dislike and all strange beasts lie down together where the newborn child is. It is love of this kind, passionate yet dispassionate love, that leads a man to accomplish what Laotze says when he asks, 'Can your learned head take leaven from the wisdom of your heart?'

> If you can bear issue and nourish its growing,
> If you can guide without calm or strife,
> If you can stay in the lead of men without their knowing,
> You are at the core of life.

Well, I tried to visualize this, and to feel at the core of life, but this straw to clutch at in my desolation skittered away as fast as the jackrabbit that plunked out of the sagebrush and came near entangling with our wheels as we came to the junction with Highway 99 near Gorman. We were now speeding down the Grapevine, the six per cent grade of the freeway that descends into the San Joaquin from the Tehachapi Mountains. The contrast of the bold engineered freeway, stiff, angular, smelling of gasoline, and the soft, delicate curving creek where the rams played and the sad trees dropped their leaves in the brown water, in some peculiar way set up a fugue in myself around the words 'sacrifice' and 'involuntary sacrifice'. How much purpose or meaning can we find in what we do? If we are free agents, given freedom by God, then we can learn the way of sacrifice, of 'making holy', yielding up, for spiritual growth. But what about cancer, or accidents that come meaninglessly and cut us off, break us down, not at the end but in the clear middle of life? What about the earthquake, the hurricane, the insidious hurricane within that is the incurable disease? What about that?

Well, I can easily sacrifice my possessions. I do not have very

57

many. The rub comes when I see love as the core of life and must give up my loved ones, give them up not because I need them for myself as much as because they need me. How cruel, how very, very cruel. What, God, are you asking me to do? Yes, I know you have set up certain natural laws. Cancer, as once also with what they called 'galloping consumption', obeys certain laws and science has not yet found the cause of these malignant cell growths, but it will some day. And I can't ask you to reverse a law you have made yourself. That would be going against yourself. And you give us mind to find out these natural laws and, in time, in due season, past my time, in time we will, we human beings will. Yes, and there is the possibility you are not complete, not perfect, but incomplete and imperfect, and you need us to complete you. That's why you had to give us choices, because you couldn't grow without our choices to help you. But at this point you are literally goddamned asleep, the sleeping God, and I can, as a gnat, sting you with my death! My going will create a rumpus in the little world in which I live and the gnat stings! He may awaken you or he may not, but he stings to consciousness! I pounded the seat a little and kept crying, 'Why . . . Why . . . Why . . . Why . . . Why?'

No answer came, of course, and certainly not from the sleeping silent winter hills and the dead grass and the green grass immovable and about to dry again and the overcast sky which hung lifeless over the oil-fields, for we were now approaching Taft on the west side highway. Not a breath of wind. The oil-derricks seemed like toys, man-toys, vacantly eyeing the universe, and in the restaurant in Taft, where I could barely eat lunch with the others, the waitress was half-asleep and the kitchen odours putrescent.

As we sped on again there came a tremendous urge for the deep sleep, to lie in this dead earth and be comforted by its deadness. I tried to visualize earth creatures that might lie in this stony ground, burrow animals, rabbits, gophers, rodents, and to feel into the idea of hibernation. This is winter. I have an animal urge to sleep. Why not accept that fact? But if this is winter, knowing what I know is going on within, then where is spring? I tried to visualize how my analyst would feel with my problem. Could she identify with these little earth creatures in such a way as to bring vitality to herself in a time of desolation?

I had resolved to quit mountain-top jumping but almost by compulsion I leaped again. I am home. The girls are calling for their father. John and Eric were thrown enough by their mother's death from cancer not to have me go in the same way! Can there not be some uniqueness to my experience so it doesn't have to be the same as their mother's—for them? 'For them,' I kept saying. If I were alone with all this it would be much easier. And what a paradox. Eric is almost ready for college. He will go away. But John is only ready for high school and John and Ruth do not get on well and here they must live together with me gone! And all I have, after years, as my property, is my learning, which cost plenty, and all I can sell is my teaching, and I am removed from the family scene at just the point when the long training period is over and I can cash in on the only thing I can sell—what I have learned. The family needs that income. Ruth will be strapped without it—with a large family to support—despite all help. She needs a husband. The girls are tiny. They need a father. And the boys need me at least until they can get the bearings of manhood and they are not ready yet. It is too cruel, too unjust. And I cannot be one with the earth creatures, much as I long to sleep the deep sleep and lie in the earth. My going would only be a crippling going for them—crippling! Very well, God has his evil side. Man has always known that. The hound of heaven, the demonic powers of the universe, have fixed their collective eyes on me.

Priest Valley as one enters the Coast Range from Coalinga, where we now were in early afternoon, could be a lovely serene mountain pastureland, the friendly oaks and mistletoe limp in the soft breeze, in any other mood than this. I tried to imbibe the pastoral draught of Priest Valley, the lazy stream, the green meadow, the stupid blinking cows, and I realized suddenly why primitive peoples place shrines at the corners of streams, at the entrance to wooded areas, at the base of cliffs. Just there, are powers in the universe that must be placated. But I am modern twentieth century man and this is superstition. There are no gorgons or devil creatures in these hills, so why shrines? There are cows and a man-made road and every particle of the region can be given scientific status. All I need do is summon a convocation of geologists, life scientists, lapidaries, ethnologists, and the grand constitution of the universe here can be explained rationally and clearly to even the most unobservant passer-by.

Ah, but there are demons, not out there, but here, in me, and they have been throwing themselves about this day, January 3, in a fine Bacchanalian revel of desolation! They are all held in me now. What man once projected outwardly into shrines and symbols I wrestle with in the interior of my being. Physically there are those cancerous cells that are enlarging, second by second, and eating into my pancreas and destroying the enzymes that digest my food. Shall I then rip out this cancer and throw it upon the altar and propitiate the spirits? But that is a medical impossibility.

But I must think of all possibilities, the duration of time it takes to eat its way into my vital parts, or the possibility that it is not cancer but pancreatitis, or any other damned thing. Perhaps it is the uncertainty that terrifies me and causes my desolation. And I must live, live as long as I can, not for my sake but for the children's sake. Shall I yield and bend as Laotze admonishes, or shall I wrestle with the angel as Jacob did? All night wrestling with the angel, sweating in death-throes, winning in the end— as I am wrestling now, this day, but seemingly not winning? As we climbed over the last ridge to the Salinas Valley, I seemed to perspire despite the cold day. My death at this point cries to high heaven! I will wrestle for life or be thrown by it! I will wrestle with the sleeping God! I will sting him like a gnat! Or is this thought a Byronic gesture? God doesn't hear. Is there a God? And then I realize why so many of the psalms are praises of the Lord, despite the fact that He is terrifying and awesome and incomprehensible. Only a few, like the 23rd, really, are comforting, about walking in the valley of the shadow. In most, man gets out his timbrels and cymbals and praises a brazen God who brings fire and destruction and that's that, and all we can do is to praise Him. We can go down and down in the descent. He can bend us and break us. And, in going, we can praise Him. How can one curse, indeed, that which had given life? What is man that he should live out the lifetime of his God?

And so my questions and my indirections hauled me this way and that, as though I were in a sailing sloop, the sails set, but the rudder steered by a dark hand, certainly not mine, and the boat sailing over a dark sea.

Once again, as I had done a number of times during the Christmas season, I resorted to prayer. Several times that day, particularly in the blue moods, I found myself half-audibly expressing little scraps of words in a prayerful attempt to state my position to myself and to God. And so I returned home.

THREE JOURNAL EXCERPTS, FEBRUARY, 1956

I resolved then, upon awaking in the morning to say to myself, 'All right, I have only this day. Not the day after. Not the day after that.' Isn't that all any of us know? A picture came to mind of my two feet, walking forward in time, a burning candle implanted on the toe of each. I would concentrate upon the burning candles right here now. Why worry about the next step in time?

This was a great comfort to me, and, by keeping alive the candles, the feet, and the 'Give us our daily bread,' (by emphasizing the word 'daily' as 'this-day bread'), the next day went quite successfully, if not beautifully. And so for several successive days. I would wake up, pronounce my prayer, go upstairs, greet the girls with 'hickory-dickory-dock', nonsense words that they were very fond of, and suddenly their joyful life would become a part of my life. I would get in the car for college and, driving, feel myself into the oaks, glistening with rain, smell the morning drizzle, almost touch the oilslick on the highway, and listen hard for the flick of water on the passing tyres. Here were innumerable fragments of experience I had not fully felt before. They involved me in an unsorted universe of sense-impressions. Fortunately, I enjoy teaching, and the hours with my classes, always a pleasure were now a delight. Some of the students, the shy ones, found themselves talking in class discussion because as I put myself out to them in my feelings, they seemed to respond by some inner unseen magic. And when my thoughts strayed to the formidable future I would say, 'This is it. This is life now.'

When the sun appeared from behind the clouds it was no longer bronze. It was a liquid bath. At home the children discovered for me, through my discovery, new gestures, intonations. Not why, but how. Not why, but how. So my mind ran in a fugue with the nursery rhyme they were enjoying at the moment. Rub-a-dub-dub, three men in a tub, not why, rub-a, but how, rub-a, tub-tub. There was something of the coveted Lao-tze

61

passage in this, something of the 'glorious infant nursing at the breast'.

* * *

So I would be in a delightful present moment, playing anagrams with John and talking with Eric at the same time and watching Ruth play with the girls, all dressed up in their Sunday dresses, and the fire burning in the fireplace, and that moment would break and I would start worrying, 'What about them? How can they do without me?' And then I would force myself back to the present. The fullness of this day, this Now, is a certainty that I can be anchored to. I cannot control or order the destiny of these children. I cannot, living or dead, know what they will be or how they will grow. But if I live fully now this can be the greatest gift I can make to them. The more I am compulsive in my intuitive anxiety about them the less I can give them. I can trust my love, love now. What more do I need for fullness?

* * *

'Is there anything the matter?' Ruth asked.

'No! I'm content. I am just learning to be a quieter person.'

'I never know. You seemed to be staring off into space.'

'Not this time. I'm staring into my magic circle. Have you noticed it? I'm changing. I'm just learning to be quieter. I'm not restless or anxious or anything.'

'We have had a pleasant weekend, haven't we?'

And we had, we had. But why? Why? There had been the usual rumblings in my stomach, the early morning dragged-out feeling, but as Saturday morning moved to afternoon even these went away, and I felt strong. There were shadow thoughts about the future, yes, but somehow they, too, flitted away, like the shadows of large hawks flitting over the horizon and leaving the hills all brown and sunlit. The tall redwood outside the window seemed to find its counterpart inside me, spacious, luminous, at one with the landscape. The lines of yesterday that passed through my hour-glass of today and into the dreaded tomorrow were no longer knotted but silken and feminine. I was 'at one'—that is, not scattered.

And the hour-glass, as the clock ticks, was crystal, but its lower end, where the sand deposited, was deeply embedded in the earth. Life seemed as simple as Thoreau's path down from

62

his hut, past where the flowers delighted with their nosegays, to the shore where the pebbles gleamed in the spring water. For two days the thawing ice-jam of anxiety about myself was broken, the jagged bergs dissolved in a warmth of feeling. And really I did nothing—but everything. I washed the breakfast dishes slowly, playing, as I did as a boy, with floating the china on the surface of the soapy water like ships. I chopped innumerable vegetables and boiled up a gallon of Minestrone soup. I made a clear beef broth, the proper brew for a sprig of watercress. I played horsey with the girls and engaged in a long discussion with John on how to make money—not that I ever could!—and ate a roast beef dinner, with trimmings I wasn't supposed to eat, and drank some port wine, and had a bull-session with Eric and his friend on the draft. I was a boy again, eighteen, with them, and what to do, what to do, about this darned draft! And then Ruth and I played at courtship and the soft night slipped against the window in front of which a candle was burning. So we invited it in.

And Sunday I did nothing but everything. Corrected some English papers and wrote detailed little notes to some of the students. Made hotcakes, with wheat flour and a dash of banana, for the boys, and was greeted by 'They are swell!' and noted how Susan wanted every word of a nursery rhyme in, and if I left out one she wanted it back in, and noted Lynn's tendency to climb on the banister with a wild, 'Hey, look at me' dare-deviltry in her eye. Aren't you the one, Lynn, aren't you the one! Then I even forgot about the hourglass of time—how the passing of time has weighed upon me! Every hour seemed to rush to a doom of its own—and a silly nursery rhyme kept bounding around in my head, slipping down through my nasal passages to the quiet lake of content below with its garden-of-delight nonsense:

> Little boy Mark
> come blow your horn
> The sheep's in the meadow,
>   the cow's in the corn
> Where's the little boy
> who tends the sheep
> His shadow's in keeping
> His future's asleep
> Will you wake him? No, not I
> Round draw his circle, or he'll surely cry.

The discovery of this magic circle had really begun Friday, for I was darned tired of waking up in the morning with a despondent feeling and playing scrabble with the intuitive function in me that kept pulling me away from the present and into an imagined future, a future all too real as I dwelt upon it, as though it were more alive than today. I think I must have written ten wills and half a dozen insurance policies. And just looking at the girls would set me off into speculation about how they would be a year from now, ten years from now, twenty years from now. Not only was this tendency to bounce off into the future and meditate on doom ahead spoiling my fun, but—who knows?—it might have a psychic effect on the very real thing I felt inside me, whatever it was. Maybe there was no miracle of Lourdes for me, but who knows? Maybe the miracle is achieved by sheer powerful faith in life itself and a reconciling of the opposites, life and death, into some third position I had not yet experienced. Phrases from literature and literary anecdote would then steal into my thoughts —'joy sang in him a little while'—or the opposite, when Scotty Fitzgerald turned to his friend, in a moment of alcoholic desperation, 'God, what am I going to do? What am I going to do?'

Well, I thought, Pray I do every day, but maybe I am using the wrong technique. Now who should I pray to? 'God,' 'Lord,' 'Father,' all suggested to me the sky, heaven, thinking, the boundless blue of the horizon, and made me sad, not joyful. The connotations were *logos*, and sent me spinning off into the future. 'Thy presence now' as a form of address worked better, but I thought of a man's head and the head was my thinking, my intuition. Well, what about *eros*, my feminine side, my feelings, the great emotional unrest that drove me—for no amount of thinking would lay the ghost of the future I was too conscious of. Does one pray to 'Eros?' Too academic. Mistress Earth? Mother Earth? Dame Earth? This was better. And what did I want? 'Dear Mistress Earth, Goddess in God, counterpart of God, Lady, I address thee. Help me to close off my imaginings about the future. Help me to live right now, fully. Help me to draw a circle around my experience, a magic circle, so I can be, just be. Amen.'

'I am.' That is what the magic circle said. And suddenly all the other times when I could say 'I am' came to mind, not plummeting from heaven, but steaming up out of the lake below. I am seven and we are on that strange wild vacation we took into the heart of the Yaqui Indian country. The old hacienda with the strange name. It was owned by a Texan, who was responsible, I suppose, for that strange half-Spanish, half-fur-trapper name. He had invited Dad for a camping and hunting trip and we pitched our tent about five miles below his ranch at a place where, just above, the springs of the river came out of a white wash of sand and cow-bones and, as if by magic, a creek sprang up, shiny bright, and the sand liquid gold, and I played in it day after magical day from sunrise to sunset. I didn't make the legendary medieval castles that children are supposed to make. No. This was a modern city, only a hundred years better. A splendid bridge arched from the shore to the sandbar, a bridge compounded of stone and twigs and wet sand. And parks, using the tops of flowers and cottonwood, and tall buildings, but spaced out, and stately residential districts, and clean factories, and no slums. I had just read Dickens, whom I discovered early, and this city was the opposite of Dicken's London.

And so as I went to sleep that night, other memories flashed. 'I am.' I am eighteen, home from college for the weekend, and I am running through the woods back of the town, from a peak down to the canyon, and home. The folks had left me at the top of the peak, at my request, and driven on home. It was nine miles and three hours of running, the January ground soft under my feet. Jumping creeks, flinging over brush, knocking aside the wet branches of the bay trees, I ran. I would stop, for a moment, breathless, pick up a clod of earth, roll it in my hands, and fling it in delight high into the air. One poppy there on a hillside I still remembered, an early poppy, as golden as the sun might have been—was—if it had come out from behind the curdled sky, where the storm clouds pushed in from the Pacific, and I was running, breathing in the wine of running, the rhythm, the trees, the rocks, the earth.

'I am.' And I thought of all the other little fellows nine or eighteen or forty-seven, or whatever the age, running in sheer delight of running all over the world, now, then, everywhere, time past, time present. But I was not running away from anything. I was running as an unsaddled horse runs in a pasture, for sheer delight in running. And I was little Boy Blue asleep, quiet, in contemplation of running. The sheep was in the meadow, the cow was in the corn, and the neat arrangement of time and place that my reason told me ought to be was disrupted because there is no practical purpose in running except enjoyment of running.

I was running not away from myself but to myself. And I kept thinking of some lines in one of the Upanishads, lines I looked up next morning and they talked about running to one's self: 'He who leaves this world without having recognized his true world, has as little profit therefrom, owing to his failure in understanding, as he would have from the Vedas which he had not studied, or from a task which he had neglected to perform.' The sand and the bright shiny water were like running to embrace myself and the weekend was delightful because it seemed to belong to my true world.

But this cannot last, I told myself Sunday night. And the night descended and Monday ascended, though since the operation it was too frequently the other way around; Monday descends. But the magic circle held. Every time my thoughts would stray off—i.e., if the boys plan their trip this summer and the end comes just before they leave, how it will spoil their trip! —I would close them off with a circle, sometimes describing the circle actually with my finger circling in the air. I felt 'stretched' on Monday, not downward, but both ways, like an elastic, and somehow as though I were atop of both opposites, life and death. 'I am' was a bright thread that helped to weave the magic ring. And 'I am' was me and not-me and all people running to themselves.

Well, then, is this a kind of Rousseau innocence of nature that I must come back to? But how can you go back to what is gone? Boy nine is gone, boy eighteen is gone, and yesterday is gone. What was the difference between boy nine and boy eighteen, and man forty-seven yesterday? Little Mark, come blow your horn. Which horn? Today's? Yesterday's? But I felt a body to this experience I didn't have then as boy nine or boy eighteen. The strands of infinite sorrow and infinite life gave me a conscious relatedness yesterday to the children, Ruth, the soup-making, the dish-washing, which I could not have had before. Nor was this middle-age strand one colour, as then, but many-hued, like Joseph's coat. Ye shall enter the kingdom of heaven as a little child. Now what did He mean by that? Not the same as

66

a little child. But with still some of the child's awe, his sense of wonder, perhaps? And was the difference reverence? Then I was careless of life and unconscious of it. The experience on the sand-bar or in the woods was primal. But reverence is delight tinged with the sorrow of experience. Now I was reverent, appreciative, conscious. I knew the running. A horse runs.

Consider my attitude to the boys when they were tiny and the girls now they are tiny. Then I was always too busy and anxious about my vast intuitive plans to enjoy them at all. Saturday meant Saturday not with them, in sandplay, as it could have been, but Saturday in the library taking notes from tomes that would supposedly be distilled into a great book—which I never did finally complete. Yes, the difference is this, too. In the first half of life one must structure one's ego to find a place in the world, to accomplish goals. Unfortunately the goals, for me, as for many people, were contradictory and not according to my own nature. They were imposed goals—imposed, in my case, by the over-critical, intellectual, professorial academic mores of our time that encouraged note-desk work and compilations rather than poetic sand-work. Now my attitude, in the change-over to the second half of life, is all in search of personal meaning, not big philo-sophic meaning, but the kind of personal meaning that comes with sticking a candle in a child's birthday cake or making a soup. Meaning, or so I discovered yesterday, can be found when a child puts daddy's hat on her head and laughs with that spontaneous crackle a girl can burst into when she has half a joke to it.

And despite my really dark moods since the operation, I really have not had the anxiety about whether I'll be caught undone with 'my career' incomplete. I was always ambitious and so frequently, in years past, I had an uneasy sense of marching somewhere to a wall I must get over, only I didn't know what the wall was. Now I can say, 'There are no walls any more, no anxiety walls, and to hell with it if they change the doors on me.' So I can do the thing I enjoy for itself, not for what I get out of it, and that is why my teaching has been so much better this past semester, and that is why I now feel free to write, or make soup. I don't even want to display my wisdom to an admiring captive audience any more.

But this was different, this anxiety about my illness and the future; and how could I keep the magic circle working? The sacrifice here was involuntary. I don't want to give up my life now in the middle of raising a family, with the kids so small, any more than I want to give up the precious odour and smell and touch of the earth itself. But do I have any right to these children? And here I go off again to the future and maybe what I am saying is that I want to find meaning in this, and Lord, God, Mistress, Madame, whoever you are, you in me, and you out of me, let us use the magic circle to circumscribe my experience now, right now, and at the same time, to find the impelling urge to making a meaning, a purpose, that all will not slip away helter-skelter, like a collapsing house of cards.

My entelechy, the seed in my being that unfolded to the plant, to the flower, and to the harvest that is me, this 'I am,'—why have I sought it always through the shadowy dark periods? Perhaps, too, the harvest can be discovered in the bright periods of sun dazzle on the stream of experience. Is the unity, the thread that connects these unselfconscious periods of my youth—the sandbox, the running, and the conscious joy of yesterday—a perception of the white flame of life that runs through the universe, before me, after me, and which I for a time dip into, like bathing in a stream, in an act of baptism? You must be reborn again. Am I reborn, with the new delight, emerging from the shadow that is between the new delight and all the older delights that lie in the stream of my experience?

Monday night I was still crossing my fingers for the ascending? descending? Tuesday, my circle took me to two other reminiscences. First, I was with people everywhere now, going-to-bed people in San Francisco, getting-up people in China, noon people in Europe, and I visualized the innumerable river drops of humanity all performing their daily ablutions in the face of life. A Burmese peasant and his wife were eating rice with chopsticks, preparatory to going out to the rice-fields. And so on. It was, of course, an endless reminiscence, but I seemed to be with each of them and, being married, tended to think of them all as couples. Couples as in Plato's two halves, with a dim memory of having been complete, coupled completely, in some *a priori* experience, but now, after the anguish of separation, coupled again, in bed, in cooking rice, in planting the rice stalks, male and female in endless categories of coupling.

Second, I am at a Sierra Lake, two days in by pack-mule, and the warm late morning sun spreads its fingers into the ice-cavern on the further shore and here, where I stand, a stream babbles into deep purple high Sierra water. Margaret is there laughing as the golden trout nibble at our lines. And then it isn't Margaret but Ruth, separately and distinctly Ruth, also there, laughing as the water spills down the granite to the shore. The camp is on a little windswept point where shrub lodge-pole spread fantastic wind-carved limbs against the white granite. The boys are chasing each other in and out of the water in shouts of joy. Or I am lying on a meadow, alone, but everything is coupled, the violet with the rock, the Indian paint brush with the Gilia, the sky with the field, the granite with the soft black earth beneath the heather, and the broad current is flowing through me, the strands weaving and changing, as the water-reeds change in the lake where the stream tumbles in, and I am a hundred little brooks trembling through the meadow, all seeking a common source, the lake, the centre, the place where the many become one.

But I am one, too, with the deep-dyed strand, the sorrow and the sadness of the pines that troubled me, as a young married man, in the mountains. The sigh then had a premonition of death and often I would run out of the trees and onto the beach, where the sigh disappeared in the bright swish of the wavelets. Here, then, is the difference between sorrow and anguish. For anguish is the cry of lonely, frightened, personal, anxious pain, and sorrow is the knowledge of the deep void, the purple void that is the silent lake. The sun may gild it but the gilding is deceptive. Beneath lurk the shadows, with the sunray, and the shadows are the sorrow that stains the universe, and is that why purple is the sign of royalty? Is it that we are rich, royal, when we know the purple, accept it, even delight in it, as part of the many strands of experience?

God—Father—Lord, that is the void, the silence, the all. The magic circle is what I am, my experience circumscribed, bounded only by what is really myself when I come to myself. Is the shadow of God in the speaking and God himself in the no-speaking? A prayer began to take shape now. Don't worry about the poem as poem. Let it come as it comes.

What belongs to me, alone to me, God
And what belongs to you?
How may I know when my voiced prayer
Meets thy speechless stone and purple void?
Mine, a vine whose tendrils fail the moon
Thine, a field too vast for sight
Mine a ship that glides the gilded sea
Thine a sea too vast for compass reach
Mine the human voices I can hear
Thine the voiceless inner ear
Mine the circle, my design
What's uncircled, is that thine?

And so on my knees this Tuesday night I said my new prayer
and I ended, 'Father-Heaven, Madame-Earth, two halves in
one, thank you, thank you, thank you. Amen.' And I added as a
kind of after thought, 'It is more blessed to give than to receive.'
And I pondered. What did I do that I gave more than I received? And then I thought to myself, the paradox could be
resolved as the mystic said: 'Be thou thyself and I shall be thine.'
Is that an answer from the measureless, silent, purple void?

JOURNAL, MARCH, 1956

Last night was my darkest hour, the midnight hour, when I
could not sleep, and the jaundice with the itch returned and I
lay there for seeming hours in despair, trying to talk to God, to
reach out to Him, to find a way in the darkness. The virus that
attacked me has really hit me hard.

So I talked to Him aloud. I went all over my case, the children,
Ruth, my family, and their need for my salary, my feeling that
I have reached the point of maturity where I could really serve
impersonally the larger or the more, and the work, the great work
I thought I had accomplished going to the other side of consciousness. I must have talked an hour or more off and on. And
there was no answer, only the darkness and the stillness. I
promised and entreated. And then I knew that one must go
where 'no hope is, for it would be hope for the wrong thing,
where no love is, for it would be love for the wrong thing,' to the
darkness that is God, where the light might be, and the stillness
and the dancing. I tried to evoke my transforming symbols, God

comforting me and working over my body, the redwood tree with Jesus on it in the circle, the contemplation of the circle itself, for in my beginning is my end, the cloud of unknowing. I felt that I had touched the bottom of something, certainly despair and blackness.

And today there is sorrow, sorrow in me, and in Ruth, for she, poor soul, must travel this road partly with me, though much of it is an alone and a dark way. I know now that it is only out of the darkness I can bring anything, if I can bring it, not to be used, but only that I may find peace in the great ocean of the soul of which I am but an island.

III

The Inward View

———◆———

Mark Pelgrin took upon himself the burden of psychotherapy not because he was a miserable misfit out of step with his world. Rather fate's presentation of such facts as Margaret's cancer (not to mention his own childhood of acne and isolation) began to press at him for meanings and purposes. And he found them hard to come by. Being a thoughtful and sensitive man his tendency, although he pulled back from it mightily at times, was to reach toward more than surface or symptom healing. For quite a long period after his first seminar experiences, he relied almost entirely on self-analysis, aided by a few talks with Fritz Kunkel and by Dr. Kunkel's books. Later, the works of Dr. C. G. Jung took a major place in Mark's thought; and when time and circumstance permitted, he went into Jungian analysis.

This is not a book on analysis—but as it is a book about a man meeting death, and as a profound self-searching helped him so to do, it seemed inconceivable not to include his ways of working at analysis. Much, of course, has had to be cut from his intimate journals. What remains, we hope, will in some measure convey the devoted work on self, on dreams, on outer events, which goes into such an undertaking. For Mark, as for many people in analysis, the analytical work is one fundamental implementation of the religious journey. Mark felt that, if he were to be able to follow the teachings of Jesus as he had seen them in the seminar studies of the Synoptics, he had to know himself. Self-knowledge therefore had to be struggled for as a part

72

*of the will of God. This section will then, perhaps, reveal at a deeper
level some of the reasons why Mark could encompass his 'time to
die'.*

THREE EXCERPTS FROM JOURNAL WRITTEN
DURING SEMINARS, 1947–1949

Key—Immersion in one's past self:

This morning I resume the attempt to relive my journey, to
enact my fairy tale, for it is myself I am after, the inner self that
is distraught in many selves. Some objective questions are these:
What is the cause for my sudden emotional outbursts (and the
desires for hidden release into alcohol)? Why the ups and downs
in mood when I create? Why is there blockage of my writing flow
and my speaking flow, so that meaningless word patterns emerge?
Whence comes my picking up of ideas and regurgitation without
digestion, which leads to obscurity and antithetical statements
that have no unity? What is the cause of my indecision, my
leaning on others, my refusal to take responsibility at critical
moments?

I should not strive to re-enact this journey artificially; always
my intent should be to call up events and ideas naturally from
the unconscious, for I am weighted, like most of Western man,
on the rational, non-emotional, cause-and-effect, fact-and-result
side.

*   *   *

A sharp incident to dwell on this morning is my first recollec-
tion of wanting to write. One day at the age of seven I was in bed
all day for some minor childhood illness. I wrote a little story
called 'The Journey of the Leaf'. I don't remember the details
but the leaf travelled to Austria which I thought was Australia,
down a river to a great ocean. Obviously a number of factors
came together. The dramatic family pronouncement was I must
be a writer. This goal stuck with me—not to write, but to be a
Writer. The two are vastly different. The one is creative process,
the other is final goal. Later the desire to write became a device
to show my superiority over my fellow playmates with whom I
found it difficult to play and be at ease. Hence the beginning of
the making of a bookish person. Suppose the twist of events
should have been different. Would I have been like my father, a

labourer? More important, would I have been a more craft-handed person? I am utterly incapable of fixing things around a house!

My past seems like a cold mathematical relationship of events. There must have been strong emotions. Where were they? Resentments to whom? My dreams are particularly hard to remember. I should make every attempt to capture that part of the journey that is written in dreams. There seems to be in my dreams a constant recurrence of one image—the sea, the ocean, or the lake. This is the symbol of the unconscious. Frequently it washes up in waves over me and I am near to being drowned.

*   *   *

It is in the second half of life, Jung says, that we feel compelled to start on the new life, to start on the journey. This is because the dominant parts in us have carried us to the point we are, and have advanced us in the world. We have a crisis when the part we have pushed down begins to trip us because of neglect. In my case I should strive to find what has been pushed down.

JOURNAL EXCERPT, DECEMBER, 1950

Something is going on this past week—a shifting of parts within. Possibly it was impelled by a combination of outer events. Jack and I talked on religion and psychology Monday night, emphasizing the role of religion as individual psychological experience and not as authoritarian outer creed or church to 'live up to'. The need for the 'within' feeling grew. Then there was the play 'Come Back, Little Sheba,' with its powerfully moving statements not only on alcoholism but on the need for us all to find meaning for ourselves in this confused existence. Then came the wedding of Jack and Mary in which the minister used a passage from Kahlil Gibran's *The Prophet* to emphasize the role of twoness, not oneness, in marriage . . . for no two people are one, and growth in marriageness is twoness in oneness.

I had a sudden realization, after talking with this minister, that demanding a life after death in some kind of world of angelegos, each going on forever living as he had on earth only with the halo of a painted beatitude, is typical of that crudity in religious orientation so characteristic of Western man. How much more earthly and wise it is to 'enter the narrow gate' here, within the short span allotted for conscious fulfillment, for completeness of self. And I begin to see that 'religiosity' (the feeling of related-ness, reverence, awe, before the Fact of Life) is not a matter of space and time but a beyondness through relatedness to God, to one's self, and to others.

LETTER TO ANALYST, 1950

You asked me to write you—particularly in the off moments when I have my 'Id' bagged. The sentence itself (my being an English teacher) is a restricture. But I am worried about the con-flict in myself between the ideal of the complete man (which sub-ject I develop completely in my courses as the need for whole-ness), and the incomplete man that is myself. It is damned hard for any man to look into the well, to go upward by descending. 'Upward,' to an intuitive person like me, is very clear. It is not Y.M.C.A. It is helping people, sacrificing, taking joy in the now, accepting life, 'pious' in the sense of contemplation of the 'centre,' meditation, realization, all those words we read in Jung, Horney, or Kunkel—or Jesus, or Plato, *et al*. All are saying the same thing. How to make it particular and not general?

Your problem with me, as I see it, will be dealing with one who is intellectualized. This is good and this is bad. Good, because I feel I have touched the lives of many young people with dispassionate interpretations of the meaning of the classics of civilization in terms of my understanding of the humanities. Bad, in the sense of my personal feelings of hypocrisy. Herein lies the split personality.

Essential at the present point, in the light of a difficult human situation, is my tendency to irrational compulsions. They are: (1) overtalking, teachers' occupational disease. Inability to listen and participate in the quiet-centre idea. Includes verbalization. Documentation good, and my main strength. Not to be dis-carded but developed by my shadow functions—as I see them— sensation (details?) and feeling or logic? That Jungian area is obscure to me. Sometimes I think I am more Saroyan (feeling) than Julian Huxley (Logic). Or which? (2) Compulsion to alcohol and cigarettes. A pack and a half a day, which annoys me. A few

drinks a day, not strong liquor but ale before dinner and afterwards—which gives me a false sense of peace, an escape . . . and,
combined with the other factors, defeats my feeling of manliness,
free will, and choice.

The beast and the beauty is my problem. How to reconcile?
Intellectually clear. What a hell of a problem you've taken on
your hands . . . like all the rest!

Mark.

'THE OLD MAN AND THE NEW', JOURNAL, 1951

'Every day and every hour, every minute, walk around yourself
and see that your image is a seemly one.'

The *old man* in me is a rapid talker, one who spews language
without care as to how others may respond. He uses discussion
and conversation to exploit his own 'brilliant ideas'. This results
in his insistence on *impression*, on dominating and steering or
forcing the play of talk. Hence he is unrelated to others because
he does not *hear*. Usually he talks out big plans, instead of
writing them or acting upon them, because the talk is a vicarious
substitute for the real thing which requires hard thinking and the
facing of detail and discipline. In this sense, talk is like masturba-
tion as a substitute for the real exchange of sexual love between
man and woman.

The *new man* is more growing, more sensitive to his own
conversation. He is ears rather than mouth. His pace is slower,
his language deliberate. He is not afraid to pause and think out
his thoughts before speaking. He substitutes the question for the
sewage of verbalization. In place of large intuitive statements,
he seeks to convey an idea by the concrete, by analogy, illustration,
joke, story, or by a combination of these things.

The *old man* was addicted to the Napoleon concept of the
grandiose and was always seeking to accomplish, in imitation of
others, tasks that were beyond his maturity or ability. These
'tasks' always came a cropper at the end. It was not until he received formal training in historical scholarship, until he was
content to be himself, that he discovered the big dream could be
realized only by the minute concrete detail.

This 'blocked creativity' the *new man*, for a time at least, will
have to accept and live with. He is only what he is, not something

other. But he will need to be always listening to new experience that might add to his 'biosphere' that which could create in him a 'something other'.

JOURNAL EXCERPT, 1952

How do you like being a human being, Pelgrin?

I like it and I don't like it, sometimes it is irresistible—you know—one way or the other.

Maybe I would like to be an animal.

I've got legs—they run—sometimes they are strong and stalwart; sometimes they are matchpegs; they don't always go the places I tell them.

I've got a body. I smell—cheese smells good and also the odour of bodies, like mine, but many bodies, like with other human beings caught in this eddy of life forces we call deviation from the animal.

I've got taste—the crunch of lettuce—and sight—I can see a star—and, with telescope, a distant star—I can visualize—put my eyes and mind together—a star that began its light years before the earth was born and what I am now seeing began before the earth spun off the sun or even before the sun.

I've got hearing, like dogs, but not as good as dogs, and my pitch is off because my dog can hear things I can't hear, but I've got tone—so has he—only I can make tone—can he?—I can compose a fugue, if I'm Bach, only I am not Bach.

I like being a human being, don't you? It bothers me. I've got response. And I pursue a warm and soft human being like me, only different, and there is a circle and a little darting thing and it says 'Benny Sent Me' . . . arrow in the egg . . . and I'm a father . . . and I've got other human beings, like me, only different . . . but that's the same way as animals, except the platypus and the fish or the amoeba. Or take the cell that divides itself . . . now there is your original protoplasm . . . there's your grand-daddy of me . . . only take it back a long time . . . but not as long as the light years from that farthest star.

Should a human being be free, Pelgrin? Cosmos, I, but nuts. Free of what? Society? Anarchism? Himself? Depth Psychology? Gauguin and the escape from it all. No meaning. Free of Pelgrin?

Yes. Self-renunciation? Step to resignation and absence of self?
Self as Ego? Ego as Self? Sounds like verbalized rigmarole.

> like the wind in the attic with an open
> window and the rat's feet on the trunk and
> the howl of wind on dead things
> dry earth in the basement and the rain
> thrusting upon the earth and the rivers of rain
> and the muddy water
> dry wet muddiness liquid
> Is it that we build tight little houses for ourselves
> and shut the doors and windows and say there is
> no up and down but attic and basement?
> Answer me! Or does my voice echo down the empty stairs,
> attic to basement, and reply with only echo.
> Or maybe I am echo for asking the question.

*It is by now a truism to say that dreams are used, in most systems
of depth analysis, as indicators of psychological needs, fears, re-
pressions, creativities. Much of the following material will include
dreams which Pelgrin found essential to his own insight. But first of
all, we include two dreams just as they were found scrawled in his
notebooks after his death.*

*This is a defensible procedure on two counts. First of all, Mark
Pelgrin used his dreams as illuminations of his psychological journey.
He worked with them carefully in his analysis, considering them to
be containers of the wisdom of the inner world of the unconscious
personality. In the second place, these particular dreams and his
comments on them were* unknown to anyone except Mark until after
his death, *when they were found in different places in his copious
notes. Thus both of them, one preceding by four years and one by a
year the onset of Mark's illness, are especially striking examples
of the way the unconscious speaks, and of the operation of what
Dr. C. G. Jung has called the principle of 'synchronicity,' a principle
that fascinated Pelgrin during his last months.*

*Dr. Jung has written: 'I am therefore using the general concept
of synchronicity in the special sense of a coincidence in time of two
or more causally unrelated events which have the same or a similar
meaning, in contrast to "synchronism," which simply means the
simultaneous occurrence of two events. . . . If natural law were an
absolute truth, then of course there could not possibly be any processes*

78

that deviate from it. But since causality is a statistical truth, it holds good only on average and thus leaves room for exceptions which must somehow be experienceable, that is to say, real. I try to regard synchronistic events as acausal exceptions of this kind. They prove to be relatively independent of space and time; . . . so that it looks as if an event which has not yet occurred were causing a perception in the present.'

Surely no one would say Pelgrin's dreams 'caused' the cancer. And, because the cancer was still a goodly time in the future when the dreams came, the cancer could not have 'caused' them. Thus it was an 'acausal synchronous event,' a supra-human or 'divine' coincidence. Mark Pelgrin would have been in accord with this, could he have had the opportunity. But in any case, the mysterious nature of these unconscious happenings is incontrovertible, regardless of how they are accounted for. The parenthetical comments on both dreams, but particularly on the first, show Mark Pelgrin's directness of approach to his life experiences. This same directness is apparent in the excerpts which follow the dreams—his attempts to understand what he really is, where he came from, what he must do to grow into a fuller maturity.

TWO DREAMS FOUND IN PELGRIN'S NOTES

Nov., 1950: I just had a very strange dream in which I dreamed I had cancer, dreamed that I woke up, and the dream then verified by my having to go to the doctors to assure me it wasn't a dream, and this happened twice. (Yet after really waking up and checking, this is not true. I do have a cyst and checked on this in August and promised to come back after the pack-trip to take care of it. Now I will! and hope it isn't cancer.)

In the dream I am walking in an unfamiliar city. Ruth is with me part of the time. I inquire about a restaurant. There are no good ones there; but I stop at a cheap one and order a meal. Then I am in a doctor's office and he is taking various tests on my ear. Finally I get the news and break it to Ruth. She is not too disturbed because the doctor said I would die sometime around 50—this would give me six or eight years in which to live. (And, as I think either of us would say in real life, it isn't the length of life, but what one makes of it. Is the dream then telling me to reshuffle my habits and live more fully, with more awareness?)

Then I wake up in my dream and try to verify this as a dream, and then I am at the college in a room over the English Dept., worrying about meeting Ruth as agreed for luncheon—and then I learn I must take shots and X-rays every day for six months. Then will come an operation. Doc gives me until 50.

August 1954: (This is just about the most terrifying and yet most philosophical dream I have ever had. It is a kind of mythology in itself.) It takes place on a kind of hill, a good deal of it, though it shifts from an amphitheatre, where I am seeing a play and these myth figures, to various places. Most memorable figure is DEATH, a Woman, who looks like someone I know. *Death is stately, dark, silent, and curiously, though I am afraid of her, I know she is a friend and that when she finally will greet me I will go uncomplainingly.* Other figures in the dream are also representative, but Death is the one they all must greatly respect. She is up the hill further than the rest. (I am sorry that this is all I can remember now, for the dream was very complicated.) Actually it was a matter of becoming acquainted with these people. *It is some time before I recognise who Death is*, though I know the others have the greatest respect for her. There is also LOVE, and, I think, other feeling qualities (PITY?) embodied largely by women in the dream.

THREE JOURNAL EXCERPTS, 1955

That I am beginning to make a shift in myself, a change in psychic components, manifests itself not only in outer action but in a number of dreams that I have had in the two or three months following the original masculine-feminine onslaught.* At times, I find acting in a new way extremely difficult. Other times I find

---

* Here and in several subsequent passages, Mark Pelgrin refers to a situation with his adolescent son John wherein the boy's psychologically 'normal' hostility, directed toward his step-mother and his father, increased during an especially difficult period of John's growth. Mark found himself almost unable to cope with the situation. This was a traumatic realization and a startling turning-point for Mark, he saw it as an event showing him his own passivity (which he called 'negative feminine') in the face of conflict. It emphasized in his mind the critical need for the development of his genuinely 'masculine' self-confidence. This he worked at assiduously.

myself involuntarily acting in the new way, without premeditation, and these are, of course, the most successful. Sometimes I experience real fear in facing a new situation with a direct masculine and positive approach, but nothing as sharp as the original shock with my son.

In a recent dream I found myself assigned a substitute teaching job at a college located somewhere near the ocean. I had just been at a masquerade party in which, along with other men, I was supposed to act the part of a woman. I changed my clothes hastily back from a woman to a man and suddenly realized I had been substituting for some elderly woman for several years. At the college, where I now arrived in man's dress, I was assigned a class of young men. I was at first afraid to meet them but then had a sudden confidence, barging in where they were gathered on a kind of porch, and telling them I had taught here once before but now I was here in a new guise. My first assignment was for them to bring in a story for next time, and I promised to bring in one, too.

The dream quite clearly indicates a shift in the male and female components in a positive direction. Indeed, it is so palpable that it hardly needs interpreting. My sudden confidence in an all masculine class, a willingness to dare to be myself, as illustrated by assigning the story and promising to bring one in, too, indicates a 'staying with the situation' in the dream, as I have tried to stay with the situation outwardly.

In other dreams I have had disruptive elements, gangster elements, that have surrounded me and engulfed me. But the following dream is very interesting because new elements and a new turning point come into the picture. (A dream is like a story. It has a problem posed, or Major Dramatic Question, at the beginning. It rises to a climax, through complications and an ascending action. It comes to a climax, crisis, or turning point, in which the elements shift in one position or another, depending on what happens to the protagonist.) Looking at this dream as one would at a play, with me as the hero or protagonist faced by the antagonist, or opposing forces, I find a number of new and surprising turns.

I dream that I can't sleep because Margaret keeps me awake. She is awake because she, too, can't sleep. We are in the middle of the night in a house vaguely reminiscent of my childhood home. Suddenly I realize I am married to both Margaret and Ruth in a strange kind of overlap of experience. I feel that Margaret will die soon but meanwhile here she is, distant from me, but there, like a shadow figure. I ask her if she has read Joanna Field's *A Life of One's Own* and she replies, 'Yes, there is something about how to sleep in it.' Then I decide to walk the streets alone, in order to get drowsy enough to sleep. Suddenly, at midnight, on a corner street, I discover what I immediately tell myself is a 'Zen-museum'. It is a low one-story building, very tastefully constructed, with large modern windows. Through them I see rows of seated figures, half-turned to me, and facing some kind of interior where there might be a fireplace. I try to open the door to the museum and find, to my surprise, that it is unlocked. Walking in, I find the figures are not alive but beautiful life-size statues seated on chairs. The statues are carved in wood, oriental Samurai and Buddha figures. One of the figures holds some cryptic words on a piece of paper. Mechanically it moves its hand and drops the paper to the floor but I don't get time to discern the writing as just at that point ten gangsterish figures break into the museum with a rush, interrupting the pool of silence. The leader is a short, muscular, Portuguese woman, who acts like a man. I yell at her, 'You only want money and power.' This does not phase her, as I hope it will, but on the other hand I am not scared of her and stand up to her. I am not quite sure whether these people are engaged in some kind of ancient bloodrite, or are there just to steal money. A big Japanese football player named 'Tanaka' chases me out of the museum and I try to hide from him in a shadow in the street. He finds me but, at the same time, I call the police. They come immediately, ten of them, accompanied by a jazz orchestra. The dream ends in an opera bouffe, everybody evidently dancing to jazz and having one hell of a good time—including me.

First, the dream indicates that I haven't yet solved the problem of my dead wife. We are both sleepless, reflecting a restlessness in me over this problem crowding for solution. Yet I tell her quite clearly I want a 'life of my own'. I recognize an 'overlap' between her and Ruth, but certainly her ghost is being laid far more than in my dreams in the hospital. Second, my dream world again evidences a curious emphasis on the Orient; and though I know in reality practically nothing about Zen Buddhism, it represents for me a joyful, mature, human relatedness with reality and time, the opposite of what has nurtured me as Western man. Quiet emergence of the timeless moment, a perceptive contact with timelessness alien to machine age man and to my over-anxiousness on the passing of time in relation to my 'cancer', is symbolized by the quiet seated figures. The cryptic nature of the words puzzled me, until my analyst suggested that such elements in dreams mean exactly what they mean to say; that becoming an individual, finding one's unique path, is mysterious, always has in it the numinous which remains cryptic and word-less. The mystery of what has happened to me this year and even before this year, can only be partially put into words. The rest is outside my verbal vision. But I do stand up to the 'power woman', and that is where the dream turns in a newly positive direction. The archetypal figures which must be dealt with in me I am not afraid of. I am fighting for my independence. Nor need the fight be grim, for the whole dream ends in humour and play as though the archetypes and I both see ourselves in some per-spective with a kind of robust vitality, a laugh from the belly. I can laugh with them, at least in the dream, and a belly-laugh is certainly heartily masculine.

Up to this point in my journey I have been so busy working on the interpretation of my dreams, relating them to my changing life experience, and undergoing what is now quite apparently a process of transformation, that I have not had time to resolve a number of perplexing questions. Perhaps they will never be answered, at least in my own terms, but here they are and they are quite relevant to the process.

If life is purposeful and meaningful, if it stems from hidden inner sources which wait for every human being to discover them, then this that we call 'God', where do we place Him? An adoles-cent question, yes, but if He is within—the kingdom of heaven is within—then the discovery of the continent of myself, and the wrestling with the inner angels or archetypes is part of the work of God. If that follows, and every human being contains part of God within, and if we are made in God's image, then what we do toward our own consciousness must add something to God's consciousness. God is not complete; but He too is in process of differentiation, as I am. The struggle in each of us for self-achievement, self-realization, individuation, is a replica of God's own struggle for differentiation, for greater awareness. We both play a part in a drama for His Glory, His realization. We bear His burdens. To put our hands out in the darkness in order to find the new light that must come with every transformation, to depart from the known way, is to take the hand of God and walk also in His unknown way. God is both life and death. Life surprises Him as much as death. Nor does this breed a Nietzschian arrogance, for to walk with God into strange and new paths, perhaps untried for both of us, breeds the greatest humility.

The other question involves time. It is quite obvious from dreams and from my experience this year that there is a whole other time than mechanical time. The clock ticks on, the days unfold in rapid succession, but there are moments that gather whole years into a perspective and there are other moments, hours, days, that accumulate to nothing but a flat continuum of unrelated and confused experience. The moments of greatest relatedness with myself or my garden or with others have no time in them. They are exact illuminating sequences completely unrelated to a clock. Is it that at these points we slip out of time into the eternal? Do these moments happen involuntarily? Can they be cultivated? In our daring twentieth century, a century of tremendous exploration, time and space become one in Einstein's relativity. The stream of consciousness developed in the novels of Joyce and Proust, wherein all experience is crystallized into a few moments or a few hours, is certainly an attempt to deal with this phenomenon. Are we beginning to learn how to break the time-barrier, as we have learned with jet planes to break the sonic barrier? Suppose one deliberately sought to cultivate 'psychological time', as Thoreau did a century ago? Or, to put the question more directly, how can one live one's life in more accord with psychological time? And not by withdrawing, like a recluse, from the real world of family, job, responsibility, but by embracing it, taking it by the hand, as it were, and leading it away from the clock and into this strange new place where dream and reality interweave in the process of transformation of self?

*   *   *

To go down, one must dig deep. We are miners, we who are in analysis, and we shoulder our picks and shovels and climb into our cage and descend deep into the shaft, where the tunnels are, the rocks, the dross, the slag, the gold, the labyrinth of our dreams and fantasies. We are Vulcans, laboriously working in the pits of being to re-forge the links of our broken chains. Our friends are the little people, the pixies and gnomes, whom we pretend not to know on the workaday surface of the 'real' world.

The descent is a precarious business, for the continent below the level of consciousness is vast. For the descent one must have a helper, the analyst, a skilled guide who has had some experience in the way, and who has an excellent memory and can remember the accumulation of symbols from dream to dream, and can listen and ask questions, and set the tone of a permissive atmosphere, and not talk too much. The hour of descent may occur once or twice a week, in Jungian analysis, and the period of searching may last two or three years or even more, for it is never quite possible for the patient to go down alone. For one takes down into the tunnel only the frail lamp of consciousness, a lamp that can easily be extinguished by mine-damp unless it is well tended.

My Ariadne, who holds the golden thread in her hand for the descent, is constantly surprising me by the magic quiet in which she goes about the business of our joint operation. Are we not all called, in the adventure that is the second half of life, to the path of self-discovery? We can refuse the call, or we can cross the threshold. We can go into the belly of the whale and be swallowed or delivered. We can fall into the womb of the sorceress or we can exorcise her. We can be lost in the jungle of self or we can find the keys to the kingdom and emerge with full freedom to live.

For nearly a year of weekly analytic hours, off and on now, we have been labouring away at the subterranean regions of my psyche. Off and on—because in chronological time it has been about five years. There were times, periods of months, when something in me prevented me from going below the surface. It was all a delusion, I told myself. There was nothing within. Man is but a creature of his reflexes and synapses and what are dreams but the epiphenomenal gurglings of a stomach ache? But when I return to Ariadne's handiwork I know we have a secret between us I dare not tell my sceptical friends. Analysis, these friends say, is 'for crazy people'. 'Of course,' I reply to them in an imaginary dialogue, 'we are all a little crazy. Which one of you feels perfectly related, at home with the stranger that is you, rooted and placed in the world at the age of 46?' I would observe, also, that most of us do not know ourselves very well, that self-knowledge, as Confucius says, or Socrates, is a kind of rare treasure. Analysis is expensive, yes, more than even the purchase of a new car. But the dividends are enormous. Analysis is not so much for crazy people, by which I presume you mean neurotics, but for us so-called 'normal' folk who would seek to enlarge the scope of our happiness.

Still, it is balky work, this shift in the mine every Thursday morning from eleven to twelve. Sometimes we have descended together and found little of value, as though the pixies and gnomes that tease my dreams have retreated farther into the shadows. We bounce back from the hard, shiny rock, and there is not even a hint of bonanza. Sometimes there are only faint clues and indirections. Sometimes we know the gold is there; and in analysis, as someone once said, the shortest distance between two points is not a straight line, but a detour.

One detour that dredged up a considerable amount of riches occurred one recent October morning, one of those bright California October mornings when the sun floods the still, luminous air, and the birds fling themselves about in the oak trees in front of our house as though drunk with the day. No fog. No wind. The brilliant light dazzles on the soft velvet of the bay, which can just barely be seen from the window of my bedroom.

I awakened with fragments of a dream gnawing on my consciousness. I keep a notebook and a pencil by my bedside to capture these fleeting things that tell me the only truth about myself I know, the uninhibited truth. I had two fragments to remember, a vague one about a woman professor who taught me nearly twenty-five years ago, and another about an elevator shaft.

I dimly felt the dreams were important. But I do not always know, when I write my dreams down, what will come of them when I discuss them in analysis. I did not know at the time that my analytic hour that afternoon would become a little classic example of the way random and inchoate elements can fuse together in a flash of illumination.

When I got to the college, the cafeteria was humming with the drum of student voices. The jukebox, even at this hour of the morning, was rolling out with a hot piano and three clarinets. And I found I had about twenty minutes before class to sit with a cup of coffee and go over my 'homework' for Ariadne. Near me, two students were going over the homework I had assigned, laboriously practising themselves on homonyms, 'principle-principal' . . . 'capital-capitol.' My homework is spelling, too, I smiled to myself, as I surreptitiously drew forth from the brief case my dream notebook into which I had written about seven dreams since the previous Thursday, some crude paintings in water-colour that I tossed off in a few spare moments, paintings from the dreams which helped me to feel more into my material, and another notebook, labelled 'Diary,' which is made up mostly of 'random jottings' that occur to me at the end of the day.

For some reason, I was impelled first to the jottings—mostly lists of frustrations that belong to the conscious realm above the surface of the inner continent. We have a kind of pattern in our analytic hour of first dealing with the 'outer', my conscious pre-occupations, and then 'the inner', my dreams. Sometimes the former may take the whole hour, sometimes the latter. On the previous Sunday I had written in the diary, 'Blissful . . . but.' I recalled that I had spent much of the day gardening. I had enjoyed an intense, passionate identification with the five pine trees in the lower corner of our yard, and with the fuschias, now in bloom, on the terrace by the redwood tree in front yard. I had felt as though my fingers were inside the trunks of the pines, and my skin prickled with delight when it rubbed against the fuschia blossoms, some purple, some carmine, and some a mixture of white and pink. I even dared to say, 'This is it, too, the centre, the moment of perfect content. It liveth in me and I in it.'

But I had written 'but', indicating that the spell was ended by sunset and my mind crowded with worrying questions. Am I doing enough for myself in this strange situation I have been plunged into as a result of my operation? Where in the deuce does God make Himself manifest? In a jazz orchestra or in Holy Communion? And there are two sets of English themes I have not corrected. I must get them back. This means working late Monday and Tuesday nights. And why am I not more efficient? And shouldn't I have taken John, my boy, to a football game Saturday? What kind of father am I?

87

That was not all. For Monday and Tuesday I had other jottings: 'frustration . . . dark moods . . . rumbles in stomach . . . occasional itches . . . signs of something wrong inside . . . all the tubes aren't standing up right . . . life is a jest . . . this is the human dilemma . . . to be caught dead in the middle of life with one's pants down.' Then came a long list of things I thought I ought to do . . . yogi practice, write a novel, go to church more regularly, take the boys to a football game, plan the long-cherished article for the *California Historical Quarterly* on the agrarian side of the gold rush, spend more time in the garden, spend less time in the garden, and so on. These I read as I sipped the black coffee. Fortunately the bell rang at this point and I had to go to class.

The sun streaming through the window, I stood in front of the blackboard and went over the homonyms, 'principle-principal . . . capitol-capital'—pedestrian and churlish work, I told myself. These tender little seedlings, these little leaves from the book of time, I observed inwardly, would do better never to go to college. Why, at my age, must I be teaching nincompoops, lumpenproletariat? No culture, no Bach, no Aristotle, not even Hemingway. Mickey Spillane, movies, television. They can't even read. Why am I not at Harvard or Bennington, expounding on 'the new Humanism' or the 'auditory imagination of T. S. Eliot'? And then I laughed, as I started to give the end-of-the-period test, but checked myself so they wouldn't see me, these twenty-seven kids, so lovable, so bearlike, so friendly. I had been over this ground before. In despising them I was despising something in myself, for somewhere early in my childhood I picked up an image of myself as 'mind'. And I had tried, very conscientiously of late, to feel that the all of me was not alone in the head but was in my toes, my chest muscles, my whole psyche. The body is me, too, like the way I felt when I identified with the earth, the pine trees, the fuschias.

The bell rang again, the little people upon whom I had been projecting my own unlived life shuffled out, and there, in front of the administration building, was Ruth waiting in the car. For my wife was having analysis, too, and this was our weekly rendezvous in roles quite different from those we played at home.

By the new freeway, it is only forty minutes to San Francisco. We talked a little as I drove, but mostly we were preoccupied with our own thoughts, gathering together the fragments to spill out on the laps of our analysts. How maladjusted is modern man, I thought to myself as we spun along the straight thick wall of concrete that thrusts with masculine vigour into the feminine breasts of the California hills. The freeway serves a purpose. It gets us to analysis. But the purpose is so mathematical, so rational, so logical, that it gets lost in its own purposeful plan and ties itself up in an endless number of paradoxes. The freeway gathers all the traffic of the Peninsula towns but the traffic load becomes so heavy that it is clogged more than the old-fashioned El Camino Real. It kills, too, because driving here requires split-second timing. One must be alert every moment to avoid death. And it seems to go right into the heart of things, the heart of the city, but it doesn't because once you get to San Francisco the ramps all spill into streets not planned for the freeway approach.

Such were my thoughts as we climbed the last steep San Francisco hill, parked the car close to the curb, climbed up the steps, rang the bell, and were ushered into our respective workshops. My analyst and I sat facing each other, an old-fashioned marble fireplace to one side. The October morning was now hot and the window open. A cable car, rattling and clanking like the ghost of Peter Donahue, its inventor, announced the hour had begun. The analyst smiled and, as always, said, 'How goes it?' I know that she had already taken a quick glance at me, for the expression on her face sensed the mood I was in. If it is dark she does not smile, though 'How goes it?' is still part of the greeting.

I started with the random jottings and frustrations, the whole damned long list that I had gone over before my spelling class, and suddenly we both started laughing.

'Martha, Martha, thou art anxious and troubled about many things,' she observed, gently. The truth of the parable we have explored before—Martha 'cumbered with much serving', and Mary content to sit at Jesus' feet. (And when will I ever learn to sit at the master's feet—for the master is life, and life is the teacher, if we will listen.) 'We must simply wait to learn what new condition life will impose on us.' But I will not wait to learn. I am Martha, busying myself in the kitchen, preparing the supper which I will never eat because I am so engaged in the preparation.

'Look,' I said, 'what really worries me is my lack of creativity.

I would like to be Mary. If I could only be content, without having to write "but" after "blissful!" If I could have the satisfaction of putting my creative energy into a content, some outer creative work that would give satisfaction! Look at those paintings! Crude! I can't even write a poem. Jargon. Cliches.'

The analyst, whose eyes chase between sunshine and shadow when they are caught unobserved, remained immobile. Her mouth had repose, I noticed.

'Perhaps when one sinks a well on one's property one doesn't always locate water right off. Yet one has faith in the water being there somewhere. Maybe Martha sinks the shaft on the wrong spot.'

'The trouble is,' I replied, 'like Western man in general, I try to make Something of everything.'

'Precisely. You are disappointed because you wanted to make something out of your Sunday garden.'

'I could not be at peace, content, because I had a driving urge to dominate myself with purpose.'

We had been over this before, too . . . sometimes in analysis the minutes tick by like a noisy cash register, for it is all adding up to a fee and you hire someone to listen to you because you are afraid to tell anyone else but the one you hire to listen to you, and when the dialogue gets over the same worn ground the cash register image gets into the front of consciousness. So, for a little bit, we discussed what I well recalled from reading about the alchemists, who were not really trying to turn base metals into gold. The better ones, like Paracelsus, knew the gold was an inward thing, and they sought to use this knowledge to work a transformation inside themselves.

'Wait a minute,' I said, holding one finger in mid air and diving into my briefcase with the other hand. 'Could this dream be at all related to what we have just said?' I pulled out the dream-book and read: 'I am on my way to my mother's, but suddenly I find myself going down, way down, miles of shaft in an elevator somewhere in the Kimberley mines, the richest mines in the world. My sensation is that it is the deepest I have ever been, the very deepest. We are going to see some excellent diamonds. Someone is with me, but I am not sure who. I feel it is a very involved dream, but it ends here.'

'This is like the mother who appears in some of your other

dreams, the mother who is there at the point of an ascent or descent of an elevator.' I realized as the analyst talked that this was a different mother from my real mother, who also has appeared in my dreams. This mother was a kind of archetypal figure, a symbol of the Feminine, of birth, of quiet nourishment, of love, of relatedness, of some value to find. I recognized immediately, more vividly than before, a shadowy female figure that I have never really seen. She exists nowhere outside of myself. Inside me, she is veiled, the Veiled One, who lives somewhere in the unknown continent.

Then I read the second dream.

'I am visiting my favourite professor, with my old friend Jones. The professor has retired and lives in a setting somewhere near the old home. There is a college girl staying with her, a sensitive, delicate creature, with delicately chiseled lips and nose and eyes, the very essence of feminity. Unfortunately I note that she has picked up some of the prof's mannerisms, aping her gestures, her voice. I feel this is a mistake. I worry about saying the right or wrong thing to the prof. I don't want to offend her or "start her off". I tell her, instead, that everyone is praising her. Then we leave her place and drive along in Jones' old car. The car acts up, all kinds of shennanigans. Sometimes it goes by itself, when we are not in it; once it climbs ridiculously on a lawn.'

'Well, let's look at the dream. What elements in it impress you?'

'The prof has been in my dreams a good deal, like all the women teachers who have played an important role in my decisions about my career. I guess you would call them women with tremendous vital energy, strong minds, acute reasoning powers, but somehow blocked in their feelings. They are all mind. Women shouldn't be all mind.'

'What part did the professor play in your life, as you now see it?' A truck and a cable car went by. On the mantle were a couple of Katchina dolls, and some gnome-like creatures in wood that the analyst picked up on her recent European trip. I stared at them a moment, thinking hard. The miner was at work within, dredging. 'Well, she once brought me to sanity.'

'How do you mean?'

'It was at the university in my junior year. I was trying to write stories, but I was trying to depend on some magic of emotion and unconscious fantasy to take over and write them for me. I had always wanted to be a writer. My room-mate introduced me to a friend who was a real writer, introduced me with the joking words, "Pelgrin thinks he is in harmony with the spheres." I realized then I did not have the talent. I was not getting on well at the university anyway. Long hours of moroseness. Unadjusted, I suppose you would say. Thought once of committing suicide. Emotionally disturbed. Werther's sorrows.' I laughed.

'And the prof?'

'Well, she rescued me from the abyss by praising a critical paper, comparing two poems. At least I can do this, I told myself. That is how I decided to take graduate work in English, pawing over the dry bones of *As You Like It* and finding in Act II, Scene 1, a line that Shakespeare did not write. Reason. Logic. Critical Spirit. I could do that. The prof symbolized it for me.'

'Was she a kind of substitute mother?'

'All of them were! The one who shifted me from my interest in the dry bones of literary scholarship to American history. The one whom I hated in high school, because she made fun of me and represented "science".' I felt suddenly very unhappy and stared at the Katchina dolls. 'Yet, as I look back, she turned me outward, prof did, from a confused inner world to mental health.'

'Perhaps she fostered what needed to be fostered at the time —to keep you from being engulfed by your unconscious. And what about the young girl? How do you feel about her?'

Pictures flashed across my mind. We were on the track of something, some clue. The young girl was the opposite of the Amazon woman, and the Amazon woman was a holy terror when I was a child. There was the girl I wrestled with in the living room when I was ten. She won. I remember I cried in exasperation. Then there were the Portuguese girls who chased me on my newspaper route when I was thirteen. They threw rocks. I was very humiliated. I felt like crying. For a moment here with the Katchina dolls, I was back on that hillside, the vacant lot, the newspapers in my bag, the bike turned over, the two bitches throwing rocks. Why? Why, oh why, in the name of God, why?

We were talking about what we had touched upon before—an old problem, one we keep coming back to, because it is there in the dreams, and this problem is this: the need for more differentiation between the masculine and feminine components in my personality. Somehow or other we have always felt that they had got translocated. Now, how to trans-translocate them.

'I remember the first time I was alienated,' suddenly I cried out, 'I mean really alienated from others. When I was nine years old I was walking down the mainstreet of the little Central American village where we lived. And I was trying to draw a map of the town, only I was doing it very, very ostensibly. Several kids put their fingers to their heads and cried out, "Loco. Americano. Loco!" Crazy fellow. Now why did I do it? Why didn't I take that damned drawing pad home and draw in my room? There was no reason to draw in the middle of a crowded town. You know what? A fantasy world must have taken me over at that point. Prof saved me from that fantasy world, and I decided to become the critic—practical, logical, in strict control of myself. I did not want my unconscious stuff to alienate me again.'

'So you had to throw the baby out with the bath,' the analyst observed. 'That was probably necessary when you were a junior at college. What about this girl with the prof?'

'I like her. She is completely passive, rooted, at home with herself. I don't like her when she tries to ape prof.'

We discussed the idea that this girl might be a real feminine image which I had rejected, a creature who represented a passive being-ness, like my fingers in the fuschias, my heart in the pine trees, my love for nature. There was another tangent here, too, for the detour in our discussion took us to the subject of maps, and I suddenly recalled how fond my younger son is of drawing maps. John and I do not get along well right now. Eric appeals to my 'mind side'. Someday Eric and I will enjoy talking about the 'auditory imagination of T. S. Eliot'. We talk even now about writing short stories and poems. And he sits at the feet, sometimes, of his father, the sage English teacher, who 'knows all'. John likes football, bikes, maps. But I liked maps, once. Could it be that I do not feel into John enough yet because he represents the rejected side of myself, the tow-headed, 'alienated' one, the one I do not like to remember because of the pain? Like my attitude to my bear-like little kids in spelling class?

We pondered that one a moment, and then came back to the girl. Active? Passive? The prof represented the active, aggressive feminine, the feelings directed by a masculine thrust. The intense outward vitality that belongs to masculinity had, in my case, been somehow projected into women. The 'mother' in the dream of the Kimberley mines, was a kind of positive helper. The girl with the prof in the other dream was a genuine feminine girl. I must pursue them further. We were getting somewhere.

'What about this next dream? Will it throw any light on this?' I asked, diving again into my briefcase. It was a dream of about three nights before.

'I am teaching in a town near Lake Tahoe. Junior college opens here a day before the regular time. But this is silly because no students show up, although all the faculty, including the PE coach, are waiting in two large basketball courts. I go outside, since there is nothing to do. The PE coach goes out, too, and runs up and down the street for practice. I wish I could run but can't as I cannot have too much exercise, since I am ill. Then the scene shifts to one where I am with my first wife, Margaret. She is implacable, saying that I am not to have wine for the Christmas dinner. I can have the turkey at the dinner we are preparing but not the wine. Everyone else is having wine and I am miffed because I cannot have my pre-dinner cocktail. Margaret has tipped them off to drink separately from me. It is all for my good, she says, for the doctor says I should not have any wine. I realize the truth of this.'

'Let's feel into the dream,' my analyst prodded.

'Well, wine is both sides of the coin,' I replied.

'Meaning?'

'It is the spirit of life, the symbol of something life-giving. But I have misused it. All the time I was married to Margaret I felt I had a wine problem, overdrinking. I couldn't afford anything else. If I had been richer, materially, I would have probably sunk into whisky. So wine is uniquely a double problem for me. And Margaret here is a kind of conscience, super-ego, censor. For my own good. . . .'

'The wine, for you, and uniquely for you, is negative,' my analyst said. 'It is the symbol of trying to call up the spirit wrongly, to force it, to force the living water. The dream here says that somehow you have the feeling that you can't quite enjoy or celebrate life without artificial inducement. What day was this feast?'

'Christmas.'

94

'What does Christmas mean to you.'

'Life out of winter dark, I suppose. Birth of the child Jesus, and the whole idea of rebirth and spring heralded in the darkest period of the year, cold, dark winter.'

'The wine was an artificial way of invoking the creativity, wasn't it? Your overly intense way of dealing with ideas is involved. There must be a more relaxed, truly sober way, the way of the young girl in the dream, who is shy, sensitive, quiet, artistic, feeling, as you say. But she does not have to extrovert. You do not like her when she apes the prof. Here is the same artificial infusion of spirit as you used with the wine. Perhaps you need to spend time with her, as well as to consider what truly is Christmas for you—the time of celebrating the new thing, the rebirth in the old.'

The hands of the little clock ticking on the mantel next to the Katchina dolls were nearing noon.

'Do you think you could formulate what we have said?' the analyst continued. 'I feel we have got on the track of something here.'

I gazed thoughtfully at the ceiling. It is so hard to say about ourselves. We half know the truth of ourselves, the nature of reality, but we don't like to tell what we know. 'Well . . . this attempt to artificially induce the spirit and therefore let the woman carry the load of my responsibility for myself certainly explains a lot in my first marriage, and begins to explain my white and black feelings about prof and the problem of my wine drinking. It is negative, all right. But in the centre of the garden that is myself I could evoke the spirit, the creativity, the genuine, not by intensity and push, not by feeling what I ought to do, but by some kind of letting things happen.'

She nodded.

'But then how about that loco kid, at the age of nine?'

'Was that such a strange thing to do? Lots of nine-year-olds do queer little things like that.'

'Then what about my self-consciousness about it?'

'Did you have anyone to take your idea to, your sudden fascination in maps and "drawing" the town?'

'No.' For I was an only child. There was no sibling to share my enthusiasms with. And I must have seemed to my parents, quite ordinary people, kind of queer. I suddenly recalled that I never went to them with my enthusiasms. They were always secret enthusiasms, something snatched for myself that I could not share with others. My fantasy world, which threatened to take me over at times, was like the Minotaur. Prof had rescued me from the labyrinth. Margaret shielded me from it, by absorbing it in herself. The fantasy world held the treasure which I did not know how to find. I had, indeed, sunk wells on the wrong part of my property. The life-giving stream did not flow fully but only intermittently. I tried to force it. I tore up pages of stories I could not write. I drank wine to give me the illusion of tapping life-giving waters. But the drinking was negative.

It was noon. I must go. There were other patients waiting. A thought teased at the edge of my consciousness.

'Do you remember my saying early in August, in regard to my cancer, that last year when I had surreptitiously drunk some wine and gone down into my garden, I had told myself, "You brought unhappiness, disaster, to Margaret. If you don't stop this you will bring the house down around your OWN ears"?'

She nodded, for we are both aware that there are strange and unseen relationships of time—synchronicity—in our lives and you may say that this is all very dark and obscure but the true scientist overlooks nothing, no fact to remain unobserved. And that I felt this way was a fact, a very real fact in my strange universe.

She nodded. 'I think there may be some relationship here, too. What is it?'

'That I will ponder on,' I replied, as I closed the door and left her with the Katchina dolls.

It was quite an hour, all right. And then I plunged back to the freeway, home, the college, two sets of English papers I had failed to 'get at' Sunday. The cares and workaday realities of the surface world. But I had another dream that night.

'I find myself camping with some mysterious woman figure. We are on a pack trip in the High Sierra and are at the end of an old road, just where the trail starts. A man comes up to us with a very big fish for dinner. We go over to his camp with him, and this enormous fish, a kind of Leviathan of a golden trout eight feet long, is stretched out on a pole. The fish is not dead yet, for its mouth is gasping for air. As it dies, I can see it is in great pain. It shudders. I feel for it, but realize now that I am to be one of the eaters of the fish. It is food we need, this woman figure and I. There is also a quiet, shy, reticent Chinese girl, similar to the girl in the dream with prof. She likes the idea of my eating the fish. I am to be married to this girl. I am to go on a long journey to China with her. The parents have some Chinese money and I am surprised that it is not crazy money, or inflated money, and that it is of exact value. The Chinese couple assure me, for I have momentary doubts, that the money has been stabilized, all right. The fish was very good eating!'

*   *   *

The fish symbol appears over and over again, in both Christian and pagan mythology. The fish was the key symbol for the Christians and the fish motif is repeated in primitive Christian paintings in the Catacombs. But back of this is a long tradition, one that Eliot wisely uses to illuminate the centre of his 'The Wasteland,' sometimes called the pivotal poem of our century. The 'fisher King,' which Eliot explains in his footnotes, and the 'drowned Phoenician sailor,' remind us of the pagan backgrounds of Christianity. Orpheus, the fisherman, takes from the great undifferentiated body of nature that which is meaningful and partakes of it.

In our next session, my analyst showed me an old woodcut in a book on psychological growth, a woodcut taken from *The Book of Lambspring*, 1625. Two enormous fishes were floating on the water of a bay. Under the woodcut was the inscription, 'The Sea is the body, the two fishes are the soul and the spirit.'

And what about my Chinese girl? Well, just how did I feel about China? How did I like Oriental paintings? 'Very much,' I replied. And, for a boy raised in the San Francisco Bay area, it was natural that childhood trips to Chinatown would evoke the feeling of the strange, the irrational side of ourselves. The words that came to my mind for China were 'mysterious . . . quietness . . . harmony . . . simplicity . . . not cluttered . . . harmony, particularly, and relatedness.' So here was a shy, quiet side of myself that needed cultivating. Laotze and Zen Buddhism particularly were not systems of belief but directions to what is essential in time. In a Chinese painting a chrysanthemum is not surrealist, some crazy design with philosophical overtones, but simply something that is, a chrysanthemum. A bush with a bird on it is a bush with a bird on it. Not a bush and bird you make something out of, but a direct experience with life, a finding of eternity in the moment.

And what about the money in the dream, the money that the Chinese parents assured me is all right, is 'stabilized'? I felt, at first, it was 'crazy' money, and in the dream I have to be assured that it has a direct and solid quality. It must have nothing inflated about it, like my vast intuitive anxieties. Money can be a stable energy unit, and was here the stable side of myself which could help to overcome my onesidedness. The whole dream also seemed to hold a clue to my personal illness problem, and 'science says'. For we know too much about science and not enough about what science doesn't know. I was again reminded of my need for dealing with IT from the irrational side, the side that lay close to the unconscious.

And perhaps what was most amazing were the after-effects of this particular analytic hour. My dreams hit a new note in feminine differentiation. A woman, unseen, but there all of the time, appeared in many of them, a kind of archetypal Mother, a nourishing creature vaguely associated in my feelings with my analyst, but I never saw the veiled figure. Two other types of women haunted my dreams, a tall, brunette, Amazonish woman, and a reticent, very feminine Chinese girl.

I felt a new power, too. 'What do you do when you have what you say is an illumination in analysis?' I can hear some sceptical friend asking. 'So what?' Well, for one thing you know something you did not know before. Playing with my new illumination, turning it over in my spare moments, as I drove to and from the college, or to the market, or as I was working in the garden or going to sleep at night, all kinds of new relationships from my past would come into my vision. If most of the key decisions in my life had been decided with the help of a certain kind of intellectual woman, an 'Amazon', as I called her, then what would that have to do with my 'objectivity', my attitude to ideas? Here I was, with a Master's Degree in Literature and a PH.D. in History. I had always heard that one could not really be objective unless he knew himself. Here, indeed, was visible proof, at least for myself, of the way in which psychic dislocations within one can govern one's attitude to a presumably objective field like dealing with facts and concepts in history. I was a liberal, a reformer type of historian, with a bias to what I called 'Jeffersonian agrarianism'. I was suspicious of masculine power, 'practical men', and particularly Big Business and the forces of 'entrenched capitalism'. I had the uneasy feeling now that if I had been born into a socialist or communist society I would have had the same attitude to the Soviet 'bosses' or the socialist 'bosses' as I had to the lobbyists for the NAM, etc. Why? The answer must lie somewhere in my own interior arrangements of things. Not that a man of consciousness, of integrity, does not deal honestly with outer evil where he sees it; (with, in my own time, the fanatical eruption of extreme reactionaryism of Mc-Carthyism;) but, deep within, there are emotional wellsprings for one's belief that have their roots in the unconscious, and the bringing of these to the conscious light of day could help enormously in the achievement of some objectivity in human affairs. What, then, was truly and objectively honest in my attitude to society? What was subjectively tied to the apron strings of the inner goddess?

Here, indeed, was food for reflection, and I started lists. When could I first date my discovery of history? Of a magnetic attraction to protest against the established order of things? Was this really a fruit of the depression, as it was for many of my contemporaries? The fruit of a natural American agrarian protest against power and capitalism and authority? Or did it spring from certain personal elements in my psyche?

As I worked on these questions day by day, the emergence of a clearer idea of the relation between my feminine and masculine sides began to change my habits, my movements, the ways in which I reacted to people and ideas. What was genuinely feminine, I reacted to in a feminine way. What was genuinely masculine, I reacted to in a masculine way. Consciousness of both forces working within me and of their growing differentiation took much of the unnecessary emotional thrust out of my dealing with masculine ideas. Likewise, where the reaction was feminine, I had a growing sense of a proportion here that belonged in and for itself to its proper function. For really the first time in my analysis I could actually feel, within myself, a transformation taking place. My crude little paintings, which I tried to do on week-ends, became more sure, and themes began to emerge. I kept drawing a pagoda, for example, but one with a round rather than rectangular or square door, as though wanting to draw a magic ring around myself to separate what properly belonged from what did not. Sometimes a long stairway from a bay or river or ocean bed led to the round door of the pagoda, and the stairway was frequently crowded with misshapen figures, anxious to climb into my sanctuary with me. Sometimes I isolated these figures and drew them by themselves, and they came to be what I called the 'seven Mad Gods,' seven fiendish forms who danced about carelessly and recklessly in my 'within' country.

Mark spoke truly when he wrote that all kinds of new illuminations were coming to him, and that he was in fact changing. The rush of these illuminations is evidenced in the preceding sketches of his analytic progress, where dreams and ideas and questions and more dreams are piled upon each other in profusion. The fullness of his dealing with all these elements is not really conveyed in his diary-journal, of course. And as his time shortened, his work at himself intensified. He entered ever more deeply into the 'foreign lands' in himself, and found that he was neither clumsy nor insensitive. He began to acknowledge who he really was.

The dream immediately following shows in a rather clear way some of these trends in Mark. Then his journal excerpts continues to elaborate them, most especially that trend which moved him toward his greater 'manhood', as he called it.

'We are travelling in a foreign country. I have only three days so must crowd in as much as I can. We are travelling in some town, and want to get on to the capital, so we finally, after much difficulty, get a bus. Unfortunately, we learn as we begin crossing a desert that the bus is going to a town in Spain. So we get off and get on another bus which is going to Holland. We get off at Amsterdam, smallish town by sea, no canals, and I am puzzled. After going through this town, we leave ocean and bay, and come to a park. There is a fellow there who says I am quite polite for an American. I thank him. I give him my address and tell him I am from California. He praises me for being perceptive.' (Note, a number of dreams this week much in spirit not of self-condemnation but of praise. How does one figure!)

FOUR JOURNAL ENTRIES FROM NOVEMBER, 1955

There seem, then, to be two parts of me—the masculine and the feminine. The masculine, instinctually, is decisive in tone and attitude, thrusting. It does not shilly-shally. In the case of my son John I should not be afraid. We have this or that, or we don't have this or that, and I am brief and to the point. It must be very important that I am not afraid to tell him what's what, in direct words, and the fewer words the better. I directly confront him like a man. Whatever discipline there is to be done with the boys, I do. Ruth should not be the goat for discipline. It doesn't do ME any good for her to play the role of the disciplinarian.

Now the feminine side is relatedness, sensitivity to the feelings. Women are relationship creatures. Relating to femininity means relating to actuality, not an idea about reality, or an abstraction of reality. An outdoor rugged man may be very masculine and yet tender in his relationships to himself and other people, in his awareness of others.

But, for me, women have carried the masculine principle. The feminine principle for me has not been feminine but masculine. Note that in music the really great composers are masculine, like Bach, etc. Feminine men have not written the greatest music. The problem is man not relating to the masculine, to his potency. If his potency isn't there, he is not a great artist.

So I will try to keep a record of changes in myself, in my attitudes, to know whether there is any shift in myself as a result of my insight. For instance, I felt much more understanding with Carl Tiflin, in Steinbeck's *The Red Pony*, the other day in teaching. Before, I never thought much of him, describing him to myself as an 'unrelated father'. Now I see that he has his place, too. He sets the pattern of authority in which Jody can be comfortable. Maybe he didn't understand the feelings of a boy, as Buck says, but he had to be there for Jody's archetypes to be all in place.

All this material of my masculine-feminine sequence of dreams is fascinating in the light of this question: What happens in analysis to yourself? So what? When you get an insight, what do you do with it? I have discovered so far that the insight impels one to a change. It is not just a 'mere insight'. Something within the unconscious is there at work moving one's self around, as it were. Actually, it is not a question of what one DOES with an insight but actually the fact that things 'do it' to us. If we look at things in life that happen to us as if they are dreams, requiring our interpretation and examination, and if dreams are indirect ways to say something about ourselves in relation to life and to people around us, then the interaction is quite clear.

So I am the laboratory for a scientific expedition conducted by me. One answer to the question, 'How do we know what happens in analysis?' is, 'By the way we relate to those we love, including ourselves.' Now to myself I have to bring a combination of work and prayer. The roots of the word 'laboratory' are 'labore', work, and 'oratorium', prayer-place. Work in the prayer-place. The work, the patient, deliberate attempt to follow myself around in order to understand myself, is clear. Prayer is the attitude I must take, not of jesting at myself as I once did, not of making fun of the ridiculous situation I am in, but of taking seriously 'the work'. He who prays has a great work. He who works has a great prayer. (This new faith is beginning to creep into my attempts at poetry, particularly when I avoid philosophical and abstract words and ideas, and go in for poetry as sensory reporting.)

This week, following the 'great dreams' week, I have had no dreams at all. Why not? Could it be that my unconscious wants to say that these things must be actualized? In my gold mine dream and my fish dream I have a heck of a lot to work on, transferring new attitudes and discoveries to reality.

It is important that I not verbalize this falsely, that I keep my writing clean and honest. Much is not put into words that is connected with the 'laboratory'. Dreams, like real poetry, are the opposite of intellectualism. The Eleusinian mysteries were not verbalized, hence we have few written records of them. Torches were lighted and the neophytes were shown a reaped ear of corn. There they were confronted by the garden of the soul, the sacred flower, the sacred wheat.

*   *   *

A significant dream:

'I have some very nice silverware, quite expensive. I find myself in a large place owned by a Philippine family named Balusan. The house is intended for a large number of people and I am invited to stay there a while. There is an outside open dining-room with many tables on the street level, but I am afraid to leave my silver there as it might be stolen. I find myself inside corridors that completely surround an inner dining-room below the street level. But even here, though there are many tables, I am also afraid to deposit the silver as it might be stolen. There are beautifully labelled drawers underneath these tables and even here I am afraid to relinquish those cherished silver pieces. So finally a pretty semi-Oriental daughter of the family comes to me and, though she is somewhat spoiled, I trust her. She tells me, when she is asked, to put the silver in a safe place, and shows me a silver closet, very secret, in one of the corridors.'

After discussing this dream in analysis, my problem about the silver seemed to represent a hugging to my values, trying to keep them secret. Here are values with a history, for I feel the silver is old and has belonged to me for some time. It symbolizes something I do not share with Ruth, or with life, or with my real self. This does not necessarily mean I should extrovert myself all over the place, but it does mean I am afraid to use values that I have. The silver in the dream is obviously intended to be used, to be enjoyed, but the room-inside-the-room idea here means I do not want to risk sharing myself and my real 'historical' values.

When I feel I am not worthwhile, or feel guilty, I have a desire to placate life or run away from it into 'busy work'. Instead of sharing how I feel with Ruth, for instance, in the few times we are really together, like when we are going to bed at the end of a hard day, I read a magazine. True, our schedule is terribly crowded. It keeps us apart. But there is no use saying, 'If we don't have half a day we don't have anything.' Try twenty minutes— or five minutes—for relating to Ruth in small ways. I need more to be aware of the meaningfulness of the small things in life. Put my arms around her. Say yes to life. Be more prodigal.

Another dream:

'I have cancer. My folks visit me and are tearful. They leave for some foreign place and mother writes from there saying that she has cancer, too, she thinks, and would I write her the name of the special food the doctor recommends for me. Then a big landlady, like a typical earthly Irish-woman I once knew, a boardinghouse keeper, comes in. I rent a big old room from her with a fellow who is a wonderful violinist. We clean the room, or I do, since it is dusty.'

There are many ramifications to this dream, but what is most interesting is how deep has been my apparent identification with my mother, and hers with me. I need to try to be more aware of the unlived life I have been forced to carry. I have tried to live out both parents' unlived lives, and have thus left out their lived lives.

Note the tremendous contrast between my jazz side, playing jazz piano professionally through college and after, and the intellectual, critical side. These opposites I have never been able to hitch together. It always surprises people when they find I have these two extremes. I am so 'professorial'. I play 'hot jazz'. How odd! How surprising! Strange as it seems, these two are in me symbolic of two sides of my nature that don't live easily side by side. They must meet some day as brothers. It would be a good exercise to write down all the other things that have been my lived life and see what the opposite would be.

So certainly, if I write this up, it is a chapter of bumbling exploration. What I am trying to do is to separate out the feminine from the masculine in me, and discover where they got 'transversed' and where the two parts could be friends with each other and each put in its proper place.

*　　　*　　　*

In an Elizabethan world my disorder of the pancreas this past summer, with the blocked bile ducts and liver deficiency, would have been explained by the followers of Galen as 'bilious temperament' as against 'sanguine'. The bilious temperament is overly critical, cerebral, does not act feelingly and directly but acts 'after the fact'. All of this is set forth in Burton's *Anatomy of Melancholy*. For me to relate directly and spontaneously as a man to life would be to have a 'sanguine' temperament. The Elizabethans had a concept not unlike that of Gestalt and depth psychology; temperament could change as a result of crisis or transformation in environment.

My work with my dreams clearly reveals the need for change, and half-consciously, half-unconsciously, I find myself looking at the world around me with new eyes. My greatest lack is that I have not 'dared enough,' not dared to let myself go in a sanguine way, not dared to be adventurous, to risk myself as a man directly. I even feel there is a direct relation between daring to live and diminishing the fear of death, for life and death are real opposites.

The more I let myself live with every experience the more I will be less fearful about death.

To carry this back to the past, my tendency to lose myself in wine drinking was a retreat from daring to live consciousness. Drink gives one a false sense of risking and daring. I was literally 'sicklied o'er with the pale cast of thought,' as in Hamlet. Hence I let my wife Margaret take the masculine responsibility for the boys and tended to be timid with them rather than risk immediately the discipline they needed. Hence I cooked the meals, frequently made the beds, and did the housework, because she was 'tired'. Thinking became a kind of substitute masculinity. The thinking function in itself is neither masculine nor feminine, although the man tends to be caught more on the thinking side, the woman on the feeling side. A perfect man is strong, virile, forthright, but also highly feeling in quality. This fusion is most apparent in the figure of Jesus. Also, I have seen it in a painting of a huge hirsute lumberjack holding a little calf in his arms. Beethoven and Bach are forthright, direct, and clear in what they have to say, and yet it is all done with the most exquisite feeling and tenderness. Chopin or Debussy are highly feminine, vague, indecisive. Real masculinity does not make a man insensitive; it is the other way around.

One of the most important steps I can make in this new direction would be to value my own meaning in life, my own worth as a man. My constant apologizing for myself, which has trailed through much of my life, is a result of not accepting what is natural to me. I should try continually to relate directly and immediately with experience itself. I should try to side-step having ideas on what I am supposed to feel, or what prayer is supposed to be like. Brother Lawrence found that baking bread in the monastery was the time he was most at prayer, not when he was in the church or doing what the other monks did. To relate to reality without ideas about reality! This is difficult for me. How many times, driving in the car with Ruth, or looking at paintings in a gallery, do I 'wander' to the 'thinking about' something not connected with the immediate sensuous contact with the experience at the moment!

*   *   *

It is becoming increasingly clear to me that the man has to separate himself from the mother in a way the woman doesn't.

The man is physically different from the mother to start with. Physically, he cannot identify with her over as long a period of time as the woman can. He is challenged to break loose and conquer the Mother Dragon. If his relation with his mother was not a good one, he seeks a mother relation later, because he yearns for what was not completed or developed in childhood. If the father is around to help a boy to manhood, much psychic energy is 'saved' that can be turned into useful channels. But in my case I was not related to my father, either. Cut off from my parents early, I fancied I was 'freed'. In high school, since I seemed to be superior in intelligence, I was able to outwit them and come and go pretty much as I pleased. Actually, instead of being freed I was plunged into the perplexing problem of working out the father-mother relationship in me by myself, rather than through them, as if they were ghostly presences.

The ghosts and 'haunts' of primitive man are very real symbols of inner processes. A primitive will explain, 'This man is sick because he is possessed by the ghost of his mother, or his wife.' The ghost can only be laid by magic charms and rites. On a psychological level, a man possessed by some mother he is looking for, some woman figure who will carry his own masculine creativity, *is* sick.

Why can I not let the ghosts lie? If I go about stirring up these ghosts in my personal unconscious, won't I be stirring up a hornet's nest I might well leave alone? I suppose a first answer would be that they did not leave me alone and were greater harpies when I ignored them than now when I am more conscious. Ghosts are stirred up because they are not being paid attention to, and somehow they get into the going picture of life and determine what happens to us—as the 'haunts' drove the Emperor Jones, in O'Neill's play, to the last silver bullet. To one in analysis, the ghosts that come in dreams or in our waking problems, or in discussion with the analyst, are a kind of rap on the knuckles given us by the gods. Here, they say, are things you are not paying attention to. An analysand is in a more sensitized domain of himself than before analysis began. He becomes aware of much more in himself and in the world around him. Indeed, everything in the universe becomes meaningful. Where once he used to say 'It was good luck, or 'It was bad luck,' he now tends to look for meanings that bear upon his

growing desire to be related to the world around him. As soon as
he seeks responsibility, awareness, he finds deep meaning.
Nothing that happens can be dismissed as a whimsy, or good
luck, or bad luck. On the positive side, the more we are related
to ourselves, the less the sequence of unfortunate things that can
happen to us. Or, to put it another way, if we solve the problem
that haunts us, we are no longer haunted. Hence, in fairy tales, the
beast is transformed into a Prince Charming, or the monster is
divided in smaller parts which can be made use of.

THREE JOURNAL EXCERPTS, MARCH, 1956

My illness is deeply related to the Mother problem, I think. I
never, as a child, felt motherliness. The fact is obvious. So I
never felt life as a transforming container. Hence I took the
negative way of the Dark Mother, the mother of oblivion. Now
I must get related to the Transforming Mother who nourishes
and sends forward her children. To what extent has the Dark-
Mother-destroyer symbol brought about a death wish?

When I felt well this past Saturday, a good day, I kept saying
LIFE LIFE LIFE LIFE LIFE and it helped. I must learn to listen for
myself and my moods and then work out little 'magic' formulas
to handle the changing situations.

*   *   *

This weekend I was limp as a rag and slept all day Sunday.
Didn't want to read or do anything. I was really forced to go inside and vegetate. Then I had this extremely numinous dream,
as though it occurred outside me, and really was happening both
inside and out.

'As I seem to awaken, I see a coloured circle which is thrown on
the screen of the curtain that hangs down in front of the window
in our bedroom. (I rarely dream in colour but colour here is quite
clear.) I see myself in a reddish-brown sweater looking somewhat
young. I am walking gingerly around this circle which seems to
be black, as though I must tread carefully or I will fall in. This
is evidently a pit, the black hole, a shadow I must confront. At
the same time I am aware of terrible shouting, and evidently
there is a fight on the part of two men up the street. (Indeed, so
vivid is this shouting that when I am really awake, stirred up by

the dream, I open the door to check on this. But all was really quiet on the street in this quiet neighbourhood of ours.)'

The black hole is probably a statement approaching the core of the problem of the centre unillumined. I must walk very carefully, almost like a ritual dance into the unknown. There is perhaps also the pull of the negative feminine here, a death wish of a kind, an aspect of the Devouring Mother, a pull downward. Or I could see the black circle as the deep inner world, and I am still hesitant to let myself go to it. So I am approaching it to test it out. The shouting and the men—these are the masculine Awakeners, the helpers to put a hex on the negative feminine. They are calling me to consciousness, they are a pull away from the death wish.

The difficult weekend, and the dream, battle with the feminine desire to pull me into darkness. Who is to be the carrier of the feminine? Moody mother, female dragon, require from me increasing participation in reality. There seems to be a culmination of the struggle for possession of my own soul. The circle is a magic circle, requiring a cosmic dance, a 'walking around'. By drawing the circle, I protect myself, declare what is holy or inviolable. I MARK OUT THE PLACE WITH WHICH I HAVE TO DEAL.

*　　　*　　　*

To the alchemists the circle is the symbol of the macrocosm and of divine perfection, the Deity, the perfect form. Also the way of life leads both forward and backward, forward to a maximum degree of ego-consciousness, backward in the direction of a return to the condition of the original, but now conscious, unity. The figure possessing both a forward and a backward inclination is the circle; he who moves FORWARD IN A CIRCLE RETURNS TO A STARTING POINT. That is why the circle appears again and again as the symbol both of human life and of eternity. We spring from anonymous nature and to it we must return. He who achieves a synthesis between unconscious nature and its opposite, consciousness, achieves something which is very near to the real meaning of human existence.

The final weeks of Mark's analysis were also the final weeks of his life. Handicapped by increasing weakness, then a virus, then recurrent jaundice, he firmly held to his psychic journey, recorded his dreams, wrote in his journal. He and his analyst met together as often

as possible, first in the consultation room, then at Mark's own house,
and finally in the hospital. The religious nature of each new step
toward death was seen with increasing clarity, and the analytic
process itself became a continuous act of reconciliation between
tortured flesh and seeking spirit. It is evident from the journal that
Mark had to struggle desperately with his physical body. It is also
evident, especially from two dreams—the one immediately following
here and the one at the end of this section—that the climate of the
world of the Unconscious was one of gentle and preparatory twilight.

APRIL, 1956

A vision in a dream: I saw vividly a number of very serious men,
as though in a solemn ritual, waiting for me to come along on a
stretcher on an open veranda that faced a courtyard. They were
dressed in bright colours, some like silken jockey clothes. All
were waiting for some work to do in the courtyard, some very
important dignified work on me. There was a vague impression
of an altar there to which I was taken to be sacrificed to the gods,
to be worked on by the powers within in some healing way. At
any rate the whole time of the dream vision was very serious.

FOUR JOURNAL ENTRIES, APRIL, 1956

A very peculiar and ambivalent week. From Friday through
Wednesday I felt tired and depressed and weak. Much noise in
bowels, and diarrhoea, which seemed to be related to my weakness. Just one year ago the jaundice started that resulted in my
illness. Was I frightened by thought of the future and death?
Mother and father visited me Saturday. Was it tension resulting
from their visit?

Then, Thursday through Sunday, I felt fine. Diarrhoea mild,
continued, but I seemed to have plenty of energy. Enjoyed a
play Friday night at end of relatively busy day that would have
exhausted me a few days before. There is also a definite rhythm,
then, judging from this and previous experience, in my moods.

How come? Laid off smoking Thursday and Friday, down to six cigarettes and careful Saturday. Prayed. Told God I would throw everything into battle. Asked for a transformation. Want to see the old man go and the new man come in. Ruth notices, as do I, a change toward a more quiet, more slow, balanced, less excitable, less extroverted behaviour.

*   *   *

It looks as if I were in the hands of some fateful and, to me, seemingly malign power. In the little time left I should set about exploring this power as objectively as possible, so others could profit. The nature of this constellation is a powerful archetype beyond my conscious control. I have been reading about Jung's Synchronicity and the acausal connecting principle, and I am impressed with his exploration of acausal factors—a meaningful theory about what we call chance and coincidence. My own web of fateful circumstances seems to have begun with my birth. I have explored as deeply as possible my unconscious; the dreams seemed positive and yet ambivalent after analysis began, and after the operation.

Since the operation, there were months of real opposites, ups and downs in feelings, although I had no physical symptoms. Then in November, though the urine remained OK, I developed permanent diarrhoea. This was preceded by a trauma over a family crisis and my need to assert myself as a masculine being. My notes elsewhere indicate the course of my dreams and my alternate moods of hope and despair, as some weeks I felt 'fine,' and others 'low'. Now isn't it strange that the present recurrence of heavy jaundice should have been preceded, just as I was feeling better Easter week, by a bacterial organism that got into my blood stream and hurt the inflamed area? My temperature rose, my first attack 103 degrees, and in a few days it hit 104 degrees. I was brought into the hospital, and intravenous feeding and penicillin turned the trick and my temperature went back to normal.

I have had penicillin every four hours for five days—loaded with it. But the itch grows, the urine is darker, the picture of the cut-off shunt closes in. Obviously the infection is gone but not the expanded inflamed area that has increased. How long I have now I do not know. I am prepared to face anything with whatever courage, strength, and spiritual forces I can consciously summon. But I stand helpless in the face of a physical fact, a malignant tumor, and I am tempted to think of some acausal, irrational thing maintained by a dark power, the dark side of God. 'It is a terrible thing to fall into the hands of the Living God!' What next? Will it be a growing jaundice and more and more of that terrible itch? I tried over and over again last night to ask for a miracle, but the process downhill goes on. I am helpless—except that I can realize that positively I am a worthy creature, that I have contributed to the world, found meaning and consciousness for myself and others.

Will the liver deteriorate with the bile dripping on it? Pain comes in the end. This we hope the doctors can alleviate, and just when the end, I cannot know, but death will be from a deterioration of the vital organs and exhaustion, etc. Meanwhile I must do what I can to strengthen myself for the final transformation. Write some—poetry perhaps. I must come to know my family even more. I am lucky in that I have friends, a loving family, the help of an analyst, excellent doctors, security, and some freedom of worry about money. I hope I can last to sign the contract for next year so the family can get some of the salary. I almost can't believe this is happening to me. The 'coincidences' all seem so strange. Is there some terrible synchronicity here? The thing is, I am being taken at exactly the point where I could do so much, and I am needed so much. Certainly this new turn of things in a seemingly downhill direction gives me a new responsibility to myself and to others, but what is its nature?

1. To be outwardly cheerful with others so that they can have a positive feeling about me even when I am heartsick within.

2. To work on 'my work' of transformation, to follow where it leads by writing down dreams, going on with analysis, doing active imagination, working with painting and poetry. Finding strength beyond hope and despair is in the sense of *this life*. To detach myself from 'love'. That is, to enjoy the family for themselves but not with possessive love, for it knots me up when I become so attached to them. And when I know I cannot see them grow up and know they will never really know me—this is what the detachment of Buddha means. So my analyst and I must try to trace the creative stream back as far as possible. The word I have seemed to miss this week is 'faith'. I wrote of strength beyond hope and despair, etc., but I overlooked faith,

and I mean real faith—faith in letting it happen. What happens happens. Obviously there are forces here larger than I am. I can only put my trust in their operation, and in the sense that somehow the 'synchronicity' will be meaningful in the fullest sense of the word. I will know where I am when I get there.

*   *   *

I returned from the hospital Monday. Tuesday night, just after telling Jack over the telephone that I itched horribly, there was a very slight shift of the physical symptoms in a better direction. I was, of course, overjoyed.

The next morning my analyst and Elizabeth came down. How wonderful of them, for it meant a real voluntary sacrifice, putting off or cancelling their regular appointments! My analyst and I discussed the following points, and during the course of the hour much I had discussed before with her came to a new focus:

1. I told her that I felt in some way transformed by this one more horrible experience; that I was a new Man and felt like I had almost to learn to walk again. Indeed, she had to help me keep myself on the ground as I was almost afraid I would walk wrongly and into something else.

2. We discussed a dream in which 'bolts of Zeus' killed a 'crazy woman,' the negative feminine that would suck me down. I had drawn the dream and showed it to her. I told her the drawing was so terrible to look at that I had shuddered when I thought of it. She mentioned the Lancelot story in which he had to rescue some captive maidens. She wondered if I had not veered between two opposites—the hands downward, as though to say, 'Poor me, I am no good,' and the clenched fist, the hand mailed as though to say, 'I will fight back'. Had I thought of a middle position—the open, outstretched hand? I told her about the formula I discovered in the hospital—an earnest seeking of God as a strength in the darkness beyond all opposites; and adding later the idea of saying over and over, 'Let it happen'. I am in the hands of something far larger than I. Have faith in letting it happen.

3. We then discussed another dream that came the same night, in bewteen two attacks, and that night was a despairing one because of the itch and the jaundice which had got to a peak. (The next day I told Ruth that I couldn't stay home with the itch. I would go to school to forget my troubles, which I did.) The

other dream had to do with telling a friend about the cancer, and he is annoyed and says that I am dramatizing too much. Could it be, I asked, that I have 'invented' the cancer as an excuse for not really facing my inner problem? The way a little child 'eats worms'? I had to admit that I got a kind of secret, dramatic, and morbid excitement out of the thought of my dying in such a way. Maybe I had projected my problems, as a man often does with the feminine, onto the body. Certainly all the intestinal troubles were not necessarily linked to cancer, even according to the 'cold surgeon'. It could, he said, be psychosomatic.

4. We then went over the dreams I had in the hospital. I am a new man, with new bearings and attitude. I am now past the 'midpoint'. Some symptoms changed the same night after I had written a poem on 'Midpoint'.

But after my analyst left, in about two hours, I itched and immediately swung over to the opposite. I had been in high hopes for thirty-six hours. But the depressing opposite had come. Now I kept looking at the curtain and saying—the Middle way, the Middle way. Find it. There is Tao. And I kept outstretching my hands, as the midpoint between the negative poor limp hand and the clenched fist, and saying, 'Have faith in letting it happen.' That night I was hungry and ate a good dinner. But I itched and felt miserable all over. I drank a lot of water. My elimination improved. I kept drinking more water. Even my itch seemed better, and with my usual sleeping pills I had a good rest. This morning I itch in spots, my elimination is worse again, but I have a feeling it will work itself out if I let it happen. Ruth reminds me that it took several days after my operation to get over the itch and jaundice. The bile needs to be washed out, literally.

*   *   *

Though I itched increasingly last night, and took three sleeping pills to get a good night's rest, the words I told myself yesterday evening held and I feel calm. Not anxious but content. My helpful words are: Have faith in letting it happen. This is much like saying: Submit to the Will of God—or the Moslem: 'It is Allah.' I cannot fight with my conscious will against this larger-than-myself thing that is happening. There are vast powers at work beyond my comprehension. I can only put my hope and faith in them. I must remember the same for any creative work that I now do. Let it happen means staying close to my unconscious and letting it operate. I must remember this formula in my dark moods. Symbolically it is like myself being in a boat in a vast river and letting myself drift with the current —as the dream of the ferry boat I had last night.

From this time until the end, about ten days later, the 'work of transformation' went on for the most part unrecorded save in the inward places of Mark's being. (His last writing was a letter to his analyst. This appears at the close of the final section of this book.)

A few nights before his second operation, Mark had a dream which was never discussed but was found in his notes after his death. It is important to record here, both as a most fitting conclusion to Mark's analysis, and also as a dramatic testimony to the psychological wisdom of the inner world which helped Mark to meet death as an enemy overcome.

Had a vague dream of taking off in an airplane with a flight crew. We have a secret weapon against the enemy which we put in the plane. We meet the enemy and crash him in the air, but unfortunately we are destroyed in the process. (Sometime in this vague fragment I feel the enemy is attacked in a submarine with the same situation resulting.) But more likely it is in the bombing plane. I interpret this dream directly as the fact that death is to come but that I have a secret magic that overcomes and destroys it. Fear of it? I question whether the word 'fear' is right.

IV

The Larger Meanings

All meanings for Mark Pelgrin in his last years were large, even meanings about small matters. So to call certain things 'larger' could well imply other things which were 'smaller,' a distinction in no way intended. Yet his meanings did become larger in the sense of more expanded, more encompassing, more out-reaching and in-gathering. These he articulated sometimes in 'sermons' (not included here), sometimes in 'meditations' in his journal. It will be clear that he did not make any dichotomy of religious and psychological meanings, and that the Now within which he struggled to live contained the petty addiction and the cosmic joy side by side. This was quite in keeping, he would have felt, with both the teachings of Jesus and the psychology of Jung as he had worked at them. The Sabbath was made for man. The myths were awakened in the soul of man. Whatever man did to become Man belonged to man and God conjoined.

When Pelgrin wrote of 'the alchemy of consciousness,' of the 'open universe,' or of the 'stages of the Way,' he was writing of experienced life. When he wrote about the nativity story, he was telling how the myth of the divine child was vitalized in his individual psyche. At least two years before his death, and thus before any knowledge of its immanence, he was trying to see the meanings in the 'time' and the 'season,' in 'sacrifice,' in the 'whole experience from birth to death'.

Then in July, 1955, after his first operation, Mark had to move into the 'darkness of God'—to quote T. S. Eliot, his favourite poet.

115

*Meanings had to become even larger as the physical world con-
tracted, and the almost insupportable not-knowing underlined the
urgency of another kind of knowledge. In confronting what he called
this 'free ride,' in trying to put his hand into this darkness, Mark
moved in wide arcs of hope and despair. There were times of shaking
his fist at God, and times of flowing with the paradoxically 'absurd'
possibles. He did not give up, however, even in his blackest days and
nights. That is to say, he did not fall into the easier attitude of
resignation to an inscrutable fate; rather, he kept a firm if sometimes
fearful hold on the single purpose of bringing 'the gift of completion
of Life'. This was for him the only way through the darkness.*

*In the following excerpts from Pelgrin's journal-meditations,
there is considerable repetition and reiteration—for when a man
is dealing with such matters, he walks around himself not just
once, but over and over again, to see if there is some small but vital
thing he has missed. He asks. He prays. He grieves, and prays again.
He rebels and argues. His very existence becomes a prayer. All this
was true of Mark Pelgrin. And in the end he spoke of his 'jewels in
the dark,' and of the 'radiant mystery' into which his meaning was
absorbed.*

LENTEN MEDITATION, 1954

Discipline: The problem then is to find ways for discovering the
depth and intensity of the experience that is 'now'. Most of our
lives, most of our time, is spent in egocentric concern over the
future or the past, in anxiety as to the roles we are playing, the
roles we have played and will play in the future. False self makes
its demands upon the content of our psyche and damages the
real and warm centre of our being, so tiny, so crushable, so
difficult to discover; the rigid old man that rides on our backs,
like the impervious fellow on the back of Sinbad the Sailor, is
made more monstrous. But the anxious age we live in, the fragmentary nature of the contemporary world, the acceleration in
speed, the competitive rush of discrete events, all these lead man
away from his natural healthy demand for integration, wholeness, completeness, harmony of person.

Addictions are attempts to deal with this phenomenon. Smoking and drinking give a narcotic escape into presentness. They
appear to act as agents to relate us to the immediate moment.

Smoking accents the present by giving us a lift, seeming to excite the nervous system into sensory appreciation of the now. Drinking dulls the anxiety about the future and forces the illusion of immediate relatedness with reality. Actually both are synthetic substitutes for the real thing. I may be able, even if I cannot completely free myself from this art of finding substitutes for immediate reality, at least to deal with it on more reasonable and human terms. But since smoking and drinking are a part of my behaviour to age 45, and since I cannot seem to use drastic surgery, I may need to explore the possibilities of a larger re-orientation in terms of behaviour patterns. Hence this Lenten paper might suggest for my attention some very basic questions as to the nature of my rigidity. What do I dearly love to hang onto? If I discard these things, what new approach to the future would this bring? To what use, in small daily ways, as well as in large ways, can I put the concept of 'the open universe'?

MEDITATION AT CHRISTMAS, 1954

Would it not be a good idea to participate in the experience of Jesus this Christmas through to New Year and Twelfth Night and on to Easter, as though I really tried to go through the stages of The Way? Compressed in the three months interval could be the whole experience from birth to death.

The birth of Jesus to me signifies 'newness,' the coming of Something to challenge the rigid and authoritarian voices and patterns of the past. The compelling light of this new star beckons Kings from the Orient, men who are not now satisfied with the old ways, even if they once were. So let me look for what I once thought wise in myself but am beginning to question. For example, my over-emphasis on intellectuality. I can't completely change that . . . but I can re-examine my use of it. I can be much more the beholder, much less the talker who would thrust himself on people with 'ideas'. And, in class discussions, I can be the leader of discussion, not the preacher.

[*This 'meditation' was not completed or polished; thus its gaps are wide and much is left unexplained. Pelgrin is here talking of the mythic meanings of the Virgin Birth, of the Magi, of the Holy*

Child, and not of an orthodox doctrine. And he is examining the ancient myth as a source of deep meaning to him.]

Jesus was born of the Virgin Mary. This is a symbol of the intervention of God, or intervention of the New Thing. Its source is the mystery of mysteries. As we know from textual study of the Bible, the Virgin Birth idea was inserted later in the story of Jesus, and appears in folk tales everywhere, long before the Jesus story, both in the Orient and Occident. It must represent some deep-seated need of the psyche to find a symbol to express this mysterious advent.

(More and more I perceive that materialism is seen not only in science, but also in the literal-mindedness of most Protestant and Catholic theologies which encrust the real teaching of the real Jesus with dogmatic barnacles. Codification and creed, exploiting this great teaching and construing it literally rather than symbolically, have brought about the present collapse of religions in the West. Man has lost the poetic imagination, which is the only way non-logical mind and feelings can be expressed. This is why Jesus, and the poets, speak in parables and symbols . . . not in scientific facts or philosophical logic.)

So, this week, let me dedicate myself to feeling with the Jesus story as it begins. What does the birth of Jesus mean to me as personal experience, as beginning a Way that will challenge me? Steps on the beginning of this Way:

The heralding of the birth of John the Baptist;

The Eastern star and the wise men, and the lowly shepherds;

The birth in the manger (in the most disdained part of me);

The flight into Egypt as a result of Herod.

What traditions and institutions does the story at this point seem to challenge? Likewise, what are the traditions and institutions in myself that are authoritarian?

FIVE JOURNAL EXCERPTS, JULY, 1955

Actually, I have been given a kind of free ride. The Thing could have happened now, but it was postponed a year or two—and there is always that ray. What does one do when one has a free ride, a year or two of grace, before the close of one's experience? The cancer patient is in a curious situation. It is unlike any other kind of illness. An accident usually comes without warnings. One is laid up, one dies, or one survives. Heart attacks are similar. One goes out on the first one. Or one never knows when the next one will come or what it will do. Although the length of time prescribed for the free ride is not exactly definite, the cancer patient is put on a year to year basis—or should we say strung up on a year to year basis—and the point is the ride is free, an extra something added to one's life. Well, what does one do?

In one sense, one goes on the way one has always. A man with a job and family, as in my case, goes on with his job and supports his family and enjoys his family and helps around the house, as always. But there is a little extra ceremony in it. This might be the last time I am teaching my favourite courses, so I am tempted to do my very best, and even allow myself luxuries in teaching I have not allowed before, luxuries that should improve my teaching, like getting to know my students better, trying more to draw them out in class discussion uninterrupted by 'the professor,' and when I am called upon to interpret, trusting to my spontaneous 'wisdom'. I feel much more that I want to listen to life, to my colleagues and students, and to what the literature I am teaching really says, and to hold my opinions more in suspension.

Family life can become more of a ceremony. I feel like spending more time with the children, playing with them, talking with them, listening to them. To say grace at meals. And silent prayers at the bedside at night. And particularly, at the end of the day, to ask and thank the Creator. To ask every day for my 'daily bread,' some spiritual refreshment, some insight for growth, some joy, something that makes each day stand out among the others. The facade of time is stripped away and every day now becomes a kind of journey. How surprising life is, as though the future, as it impinges upon this moment, is laden with surprise, with treasures to be rescued from it!

And perhaps I can discover, in this onrushing future, new sides of myself, neglected sides of myself; perhaps I can be, as much as possible, all I have not been. For if there is any goal in our lives it is this: to pass beyond ourselves as we now are, to be open to change and creativity, to become more conscious, more integrated, more rounded, more complete; and this one can do by embracing, openhanded, each new challenge and each new possibility, rather than by rejecting them for a static self-satisfied adherence to what has long been established.

As for new hobbies for me, maybe woodcarving, painting—or will words give me satisfaction? Contemplation? Something by which I can combine my hands and my brain?

And, along with this, I need to retrace, in meditation, in ruminating, possibly in writing down, the experience that has gone into my journey. The raw uncouth high school Mark would make quite a story. How clumsy I was! How painful that period was! Yet there are Thurberesque elements of humour here. Or my discovery of the art of teaching. How long it took! What a delicate art! What an impermanent yet imperishable art! If only I could pass on some of my discoveries to others!

* * *

Then there is the question of prayer. Do I pray for the 'ray of hope?' But how? I know the natural laws of the universe cannot be set aside in prayer! But do I pray that in some way the doctor misread what he saw and it was an inflammation in the pancreas that would go away? One cannot always predict exactly, nor does one always see all of what is there. Or do I pray that my spirit will meet whatever the physical situation gives me?

* * *

Meditation: Could this coming year be thought of in terms of the seasons of middle life—summer, fall, spring, rebirth? Identify my ideas and moods with the changing bay region season.

* * *

Naturally, I had thought a good deal about Margaret and her death for a long time afterward, because it was such a dramatic event in my life. And naturally, premonitions or meditations arose on my own journey. Quite often, meditating in the garden, or watering the plants, I have had a curious sense of waiting for something, some happening that would resolve much for me. It might be some insight, some dramatic change in my life. The Presence, the something larger that seems to me to be so part of nature, the garden, the Sierra, the California countryside, comes when I am alone and silent. Frequently I associate the Presence with late afternoon or sunset, though not always.

There is a kind of bronzy colour on the leaves and everything is still. One feels that one is Being, as the leaves or the birds are being. I am surrounded by this Being, in everything, and part of this Being. Then comes this sudden sense of waiting for something, something that is to happen to me. This feeling has occurred a number of times this past year.

Now, what of this is mystical nonsense, and what is true? How much is this going-into-the-self journey a going back to more primitive states of man, but how 'true' are they? Like the Jewish Old Testament idea of retribution, in the guilt feelings about the wine and sacrifice? And couldn't it be psychical sacrifice? Why in the hell did it have to be real? But cancer is unknown in cause and physiological.

*   *   *

Upstairs the gods whisper among each other and bowl and toss about the spheres of the infinite, and the tally keeper chalks up the scores, but who beyond the bowling alley keeps the tally keeper and who calls the game? Downstairs in the flat finite substance that is the earth, whoever calls the plays behind the backs of the gods who play in such haphazard fashion, does it absurdly. The universe is upside down and I who walk upon this floor in my room am really walking on the ceiling. The expected becomes the unexpected. The unexpected the expected. The possible, impossible, and the impossible possible. He who loses his life saves it. He who saves his life loses it, and if I am to embrace the absurdities of the paradoxical then I must walk downstairs when I believe I am walking upstairs and poke around in the dark cavern when I yearn for the sunlight, and empty the garbage can when the fruit is put in the bowl on the table.

Why?

Because if God speaks through paradoxes he is paradox, and his left hand does not know what his right hand does—except by my knowing and my faith I can add to his incomplete meaning. I am nothing, a finite speck in a universe so vast my imagination falters at contemplating it; yet I am everything to God because although I am only a mote in the broad beam of His eye He cannot be fulfilled without the grain of my consciousness to add to His understanding. His dimension is vast, as He said to Job, and His power is infinite, but through me He lives in the finite at this strange moment of time that is in my substance. I cannot curse Him, for that would be cursing myself and that would be committing the sin of despair more deadly than the deadliest sin, pride. For if I despair of myself I deny God and thus negate our joint existence. So then, the infinite works through me and in the realm of the infinite all things are possible.

It is precisely here where modern scientific man is trapped by the wall of his rational side—for the method of science is by means of the abstraction of possibilities into probabilities, and the science of probability has to do with categories rather than unique cases. But if God reflects Himself through the uniqueness of private single persons, then the movement of self is vastly improbable, from the viewpoint of science.

Let it out, man! What you must deal with is irrational, improbable, but possible—the absurdities of the paradoxical universe—and this is the true act of religious faith! When Abraham took his son Isaac to the sacrifice, he did so, as Kierkegaard observes, with 'fear and trembling'. He was not being put through some kind of Sunday school trial! Here was involved no case of known ethics; this was a 'teleological suspension of the ethical'.

Abraham's situation was absurd! So was Jonah's when he was flung into the water and swallowed by the whale. It is so in all dream, myth, and fairy tale. The right hand of God works by reason and by logic, by what can be comprehended within the mind of man. The left hand is the dreamer, the withered arm, God's idiot brother—the mountain of ice that ripped apart the *Titanic*, the god who commanded Abraham to sacrifice his loved and only son, not for a trial but because it is in the nature of the spiritual life to comprehend the absurd, which is something else altogether.

That at this moment of my life when I am nearest completion of myself, when time holds in suspension for me a golden age of self-realization, when I in the world of matter feel that I have, after long struggle and study and grappling, reached some meaning I can give to others—that at this moment I am to be plucked out of my universe, now that is truly absurd, with an absurdity that requires the most intense powers of religious contemplation! No more absurd than Abraham's plight, to be sure, and the son will be returned to me, I fervently hope, in some strange unexpected way.

My sin and the sin of every human being is that of being alienated and separated from God, from the purposive unity of the universe. This was predestined from the fall of man; or, to put it another way, from the moment that our marsupial ancestor first discovered or stole the divine fire of consciousness. Perhaps this was a surprising and unexpected turn not completely reckoned by the marvellous architecture that is the substance of God—the earth and the creatures on it. With the achievement of individual consciousness, the freeing of man from blind collective consciousness of this long tribal period, we enter upon a new phase. The individual is the particular, and as Kierkegaard points out in *Fear and Trembling*, this anomalous situation puts the particular at times above the absolute—a particular absolute facing the general absolute. This is what Kierkegaard means by the teleological suspension of the ethical.

For a long time I have held to the idea that, really, spiritual growth occurs as a result of crisis 'even unto death'—looking down the well of suffering, facing the shadow. But now I am not so sure, because I am put into exactly the same situation. I could argue that making any kind of spiritual meaning is absurd because what has happened is sheer coincidence within the law of probability. People have cancer and they die of cancer and it so happens that both Margaret and I, within five years of each other, got cancer. This has little to do with anything purposeful any more than four aces turned up in a hand of poker, or maybe in a double deck game the coincidence of one hand with two jokers. I could say that, since there are accidental cards dealt us by the natural laws of the universe, then I as a human being must face my irrational end, and in the middle of my life, with courage, and make what purpose I can out of it. Indeed, this cries to high heaven, that I should be threatened with extinction in the middle of things! Thus God shrinks in his dimension, and I am a Byronic hero or Nietzschian super-man confronting the universal general with my particular courage, consciousness, and contempt. But this would imply God is outside me—for if I am part of God and he is partly flowing with his dynamic energy inside me, then there are two currents from God in conflict, the irrational probabilistic coincidence of the event, and the part that is linked with some inscrutable design beyond my comprehension. Finally, I could find that, in spite of science, reason, the physician, I am to all intents and purposes facing a meaningful although absurd situation, one that I can evidently deal with only on that plane. Likewise Abraham was given an irrational command by God as a kind of trial, being asked to perform an unethical absurd act; and Abraham brought to that act, the slaying of his own son, *complete* faith in God, and his irrational side. And if one has faith in God's left hand, then out of that faith will Isaac be returned to Abraham? Will my cancer go away? Or do I really have cancer? Or is it only a pancreas disease that will heal in time? This last attitude means faith in all the possibilities, for with God all things are possible including the suspension for the time being of the probable.

Finally, no matter what happens, by my very act of challenging the probable with faith in infinite possibility—which is a kind of 'teleological suspension of the ethical'—I am challenging God himself to more awareness, for it may be that my consciousness of my problem is needed to complete his consciousness. This really puts me into a situation not unlike that of Job who, in being given by God, through Satan, every kind of disater, could only proudly hang his head when God appeared to him and told him what Job already knew, that Jehovah was all-powerful. But Job's reaction must have weighed upon God's conscience because, as Jung has pointed out in *Answer to Job* from then on in the Old Testament, in Proverbs and Prophets, God promises a mediator between the all-powerful creator and man; and such a mediator or Messiah appeared with Jesus, who gave human dimension to man's loneliness and anxiety in a seemingly cruel and tyrannical universe.

But even after this is considered, where does that leave me? I am up against a wall, and if I am forced to a hero's role in a strange and mysterious cosmic drama—for every man is a hero when he is thrust into such a situation as mine—then I must enter a labyrinth in which at the end I must find a treasure in the darkness. This treasure can only be found by giving myself up to the strange side of things. Moreover, the wall in some way is connected with getting off the track of time, for time is a rational human invention, and the world of dream and fairy tale and myth, the world that opens up the labyrinth, is timeless. Indeed, the reason for living now is not because time is short but because now is where life is. So the intensity by which I live in the now, and the degree to which I accept the strange, may help me on my journey for the treasure. I must go down deep, deep into myself—my seeming self confronting what is really my Self to find the answer. And my elusive real self, that which is naturally, uniquely, instinctually mine, will have faith as I have faith in the possibility that somewhere somehow, there is a Grail there for me as there was for Lancelot.

FIVE EXCERPTS FROM JOURNAL,
SEPTEMBER–OCTOBER, 1955

Well, I said to myself, You've got your sailing orders. Coming home from the hospital was coming home and not coming home. I knew, as I descended the stone steps from the street to our living-room that I was home but that I was also embarking on a voyage. I would never know now the other side, but my hope was that I could spot out some bearings in the crossing, some sea-posts, as it were, on the infinite ocean my frail vessel was to cross. It is not that I expected to lift the veil of that mystery which is physical death. No man can do that. But I hoped in my voyage to discover some beginning, some approach to the meaning that would bring light into the darkness. I wanted desperately a mariner's chart, not to show me the continent I, being mortal, could never know, but rather to show me a way in the sea of unknowing, and to give me indicators as to when to lower the sails or when to hoist them to the winds, all pennants flying.

The infinite sea, I well knew, was myself, the sum total of all of me, of which only the surface was visible. I wished to walk upon the waters safely, as Jesus did in Galilee, unafraid of the storms that might come. But I knew that in order to do so I must come to terms with the great sea of myself more intimately than I had before. The strange creatures that I saw there? Were they real? Were they illusion? Which was reality and which falsity? Since I had been plunged into the mystery so much sooner than I had expected, I knew that I must bring to the mystery a sense of awe and reverence.

For God has to be loved and to be feared. The sickness unto death is despair. And one cannot despair of that which has given life and is life. For that way is unaccountable death. I wanted an accountable death, one I could account for, and this way would necessarily have to lead to love, trust, and faith. On the other hand, to fear God means to stand in awe of the mystery, for if I did not fear God I would deny the mystery, reduce the human alchemy to atomic dust or to the blind channels of a scientist's mechanical universe, which would also lead to that sickness unto death which is despair.

To change the figure of speech, I cannot know where the man goes who stands at this moment on a hill against the sky, for the other side of the hill will always elude my sight. But, if I am transfigured there, on the hill, as that man when the time comes, I will be able to say of the road I climbed, that I have marked its passage, that I could explain to myself at least some of my route. And it is not the goal of the transfigured man that I must keep my eyes on, for in the dizzying blindness of that pinnacle I may stumble over the stones on the way. It is the path of the passage, the stones of the way, that would be the real guideposts—not the vision at the end. I do not even know which hill of the many the transfigured man will eventually stand upon—for the ground and the circumstance are in the hands of the mysterious unknown. To change the figure again, this moment of time is like a droplet of water held for a moment, a precious bubble, in my sight, and dissolved the next moment into the anonymous infinite sea of memory.

Out of such wonderings a vision came to me in the half-waking, half-sleeping period of early morning when the shadowy forms of the unconscious yesterdays meet the illusions of what we call the real world, which are themselves fragmentary moments gathered into present time.

In the vision I am standing before an impassable mountain range with the only gateway a precipitous canyon, and there is a man at the gateway who is holding four stones in his hands, two in the right hand and two in the left. They are stones with richly varied colours. The right-hand ones are round and polished, one blue, the other rainbow-hued. In the left hand he holds two other stones. One is out of shape, curiously distorted, whitish with streaks of brown; the other is orange. 'This stone,' he says, 'you have distorted out of shape. It is the one you use to see by, but you can't see by it until you get it back into shape, push it into place. And this orange stone is a transformer, the key to the others. It is your detail stone—the one that will help you find the little things in the large. We might call it the pick-up for the little. If you use it properly, it will pull you like a magnet to the road of the true way, and not to your imagined end of the way.' 'The transfiguration is not on the hill, then,' I reply, 'but on the way to the hill.' He nods and I pass him gravely, now holding the four stones in my own two hands.

*　　　*　　　*

God uses each of us in his own mysterious way. The Muslims and Hindus refer to this as Karma—the thread of life spun for us in our beginning. The child in us is the Self born in pristine simplicity, the pure being that we are striving to become, and that we hoped to become, so to say, when we entered our present body. It is the secret of our destiny. But how difficult the finding of that secret model of the Self, caught among all the crude exploitations in the jungle of what is! Where can I grasp the guide line that leads to the Self, the undiscovered I of my unique being? The labyrinth is many-corridored, and the way is narrow; many are called to the entrance, but few come to the dedication that leads through the maze to the interior treasure.

*　　　*　　　*

What do I work for? Naturally, to live; and my life, as a result of this ordeal, would be much changed for the good. I would have control over the compulsions, and the restless, disintegrated side would be transformed into an aliveness that would work for rather than against me.

I would like to complete some of these many projects that my restless intellectual flitting has left unfinished:

(a) An article for the *American Quarterly* or the *Pacific Spectator* on the first generations of Gold Rush, a view of the gold rush; how the Marshall discovery is to us what Plymouth Rock was to New England. Then to trace the way in which current notions—Jackson and Menton democracy—were brought to the gold-fields and coalesced with the physical reality of the surface placers and the Mexican and Spanish water and mining law; how capitalism came to the mines but was opposed by the agrarians; and particularly how Shine, Royce, Bancroft, the Hittels, interpreted these events in the first attempt to write a history of the California Gold Rush; in short, notions and ideas about the Gold Rush as they have been developed and held.

(b) An article on the Big Red Scare of 1879 to show its impact on the conservative mind in the two generations that follow.

(c) A book such as I had planned earlier, in which I try to pull together the biography of a river basin—the Central Valley—and try to show the socio-economic pattern of a unique Western region. Matt and I could work on this together. I am sure he would be interested. We could easily get a publisher.

(*d*) Send some of my stories out and write others. Revive my old idea of trying to write stories about the late teen-agers in college, and capture their language, like *Catcher in the Rye.*

(*e*) Write up my experiences from the notes I have kept.

(*f*) Get my guide sheets for American Lit courses sent to Houghton-Mifflin and to Quarto people.

But all these are secondary! As much as I would want them, more important is the transformation and discovery of what is truly myself, whose primary task is self-completeness; for every act of self-completion, of full realization of what is unique in me is an act toward the self-realization of God. I am convinced of this—the need of God for us as we need Him. This is not arrogant, but should make us very humble—for we are dedicated to a great task. This involves not only more relatedness to myself and my feeling side, but to my family and the immediate little home world I live in. And this means taking increased constructive roles in the work that is represented by the seminars. But if the other should happen, I have only time to make peace with myself and to bring to completion as much as I can, through my analysis, and to make it as easy for my family as I can. I know all my friends will be appalled. I secretely hope so, so much so that God Himself will be disturbed—but this is a kind of childish and irrational thing to say. Yet, as my analyst points out, my possibilities and my examination of them lie particularly in the irrational side of things, where the left hand of God is. I must, then, in order to make meaning out of this—and my fervent wish is to make meaning out of it when it happens (if it does!)—deal with the strange, even crazy and irrational aspect of things on a mature level, rather than on a childish, bend-the-universe-to-my-purpose level.

No man can know the ultimate mystery. We never will. But a man can invest his life with courage, dignity, sympathy, understanding, in such a way as to take the utterly crazy things that happen and to transform them into a joyful and creative illumination. I am in search of the creativity that is at the centre of human-beingness. I cannot know where this lies until I get there, but I have faith it is there where one aspect of God is. All of this implies my dealing with the opposite of what I am used to, a passive and quiet listening to what life (God) says. To learn how to be. This takes techniques: (1) learning how to shift from the active extrovert customary role that I play on my job, to the quiet centre; (2) learning the use of 'the wide scope'—feeling into and being another person, or feeling into a tree, or being aware of what now I overlook—the new and surprising thing; (3) patient training of myself to convert the negative egocentric preoccupation boiling up from my automatic or unconscious self, into useful bits of assimilated experience.

I lie as close to my unconscious as I can—because life has put upon me burdens which most of my friends do not seem to have to bear. I am envious of the John Does. It seems to be so easy for them. And I still keep asking—why me? Did I not have enough of this with Margaret? What, for goodness sake, is this extraordinary coincidence between her cancer and what has happened to me?

Between the possibility of living and the possibility of it happening next year or the year after, there is a third possibility—as yet unseen—and I guess I will have to let that open up for me when it comes. Surely I am not just some old shoe to be dealt with cavalierly by God—cast off without any inkling of what it means to play a part as a human being in this vast universe!

I could do so much now, in what I keep thinking of as my golden period. My psychic energy, frequently so bottled up in misdirected egocentric traps, now seems to flow out to *The Presence* within and without. I know this Presence is there. I can feel Him. But His ways are so strange! So incomprehensible! What kind of internal gestures can I make on my own part? Any gesture would sacrifice something for something else. That is what transformation is—the giving up of one set of unworkable, accustomed values, for another set. What would be the new values? They are but dimly sensed.

*   *   *

People need to know not only facts about the world around them but facts about themselves. But the only way to learn facts about ourselves is indirectly through our fantasy, our stream of consciousness, our symbols, our dreams. Only through the imaginative symbols of fantasy can we express our knowledge of ourselves. It is tremendous the extent to which the play of images provides us with an indication of what are our true needs. There is such meaning in interpretation of facts about ourselves in fairy tales, dreams, and literature.

Our western attitude is all wrong. The psyche is not the mind alone, or a soul connected only with head and at war with or divorced from body. If the psyche is the life force that flows through me—not only my consciousness but my feelings, my unconscious, my body, all the wisdom of other parts of me than mind—then Descartes' 'I think therefore I am,' should be 'I experience, therefore I am.' We do not yet know how to use all of our psyche in experience, but we close off much of the world by our blind mind which can see ideas about the universe but can never experience it directly. Locke, with his sensate experience, got on the right track but he got off it again.

*   *   *

Words are only little fragments that ride on top of my feelings at the crown of my head. They are jetsam floating on the sea of my feelings and why make it hard for my analyst and she has enough to do as it is but this past two days all the negative stuff erupted again. I get tired more easily than I used to do before the operation. And I think it is a crying shame, a dirty trick, to be put in this position. And I have a horror of being engulfed by death, extinguished in a few months, ahead of schedule and why should I be given this schedule anyway? The universe must be flatly indifferent to me and my family and my fellow human beings to let such a thing happen.

If I am going to be drowned, if I am going to be drowned, if I am going to be drowned, why, in the name of the seven mad gods who rule the sea, was I allowed to come thus far and contemplate the sand dunes and the ruins and the broken stones?

Do not the seven mad gods and the seventy times seventy moving forces that circumnavigate around the universe that is my consciousness know that Lynn and Susan need a father in their tiny crepuscular years ahead? That taking care of such a big house and supporting the children and having the courage to meet life will tax Ruth beyond her endurance, even though she has great reserves in her power? Do the seven mad gods not know that John and Eric had enough when their mother died, and that my drowning would put them in the vortex of incomprehensibility? Do not the seven mad gods know that I have reached a point in my career when I can be of great service to my fellow men in my humble capacity of teacher of literature in a small college? Do they not know I am not ready to drown, that there are elements in the interior continent about to be discovered? A new geography? A new map? A new direction? They must be mad gods, indeed, to create such discordance when harmony is possible!

The Upanishads say that he who sees only variety and not unity dies many deaths. He who sees unity lives forever. I do not understand this. I yearn to see unity, to find the inner Atman that seeks reconciliation with the outer Brahman. This I see briefly when I am unconscious of self, say, in my garden, and I try to feel I am IN the redwood tree, in the bird, and that we are one. But I am an individual, a single private person, a unique creature, as we are all unique creatures, and, like Ahab in *Moby Dick*, all of my frustrations are gathered into a monomania—the singleness of purpose of wanting to live. But, unlike Ahab, I am not crazy enough to want to destroy the white whale. I merely want it to leave me alone for a while. I want lots of time to be reconciled to it, to the vast, unknown, dazzling blank of whiteness that is the universe. My senses, my consciousness, my unconscious, my Self, can only bear mature fruit if I am given time. Don't the seven mad gods know that?

And, if it happens, or if it should happen soon, what a stupid, ambiguous, unrelated paradox! The only satisfaction I can get is that it will raise a stink to high heaven, literally. People will whisper and nod and talk with each other. 'Did you know about Mark Pelgrin? Isn't is sad? How awful! Leaving his wife and the children like that in the middle of his career. He knew all the time, too. A brave fellow. I can't explain it. This kind of thing happens. Yes, there is no justice. Insurance? Not much. Strange, isn't it? Just goes to show what can happen. Makes one think he ought to go to a doctor once a year for a check-up.'

People will talk. It will get around. And perhaps for a moment, just for a moment, the seven mad gods will pause in their senseless cavorting and will listen a bit and act kind of surprised at what they have done and wonder why it created so much misery and they will even be affected for a tiny, tiny miniscular fraction of an infinitesimal moment—and then plunge on heedlessly, while the next victim drowns.

This is not the way the Upanishad has it. But to believe in the

Upanishad one must practice yoga, and I am a western man and I would drown in yoga. Furthermore, I have to earn my salary this year and support my family and yoga is for rich men or for poor Hindu mendicants. Grant me the gift that pierces the veil of mystery, says the Katha Upanishad. When the wise man through spiritual concentration rests his mind on God, God that is beyond time, hard to be seen, dwelling in the mystery of things and in the heart of man, then he rises above joy and sorrow. And the majesty of God's power—life—carries away priests and warriors, and death itself is carried away.

So I contemplate life. I lie here on the bed, I sit in the garden, and I contemplate life—life flowing through my vitals, inching up with every tiny blade of grass, every bush in the garden, potential life in the wombs of my daughters who may some day carry some fragment of me forward, and life triumphs over death, and I try to become identified with life, with the flowering hydrangea outside of my windows; I try to realize the truth of the Upanishad, '. . . and death itself is carried away.' I am all men caught in the wheel of time, seeking the immanent and the transcendent. But I am full of self-pity, too. This that has happened to me has happened to no other member of our little faculty of ninety members. Except for Margaret, I have never known a case like this. The seven mad gods who seem to rule the universe come between me and Brahman.

Very well; 'A mortal lives not through breath that goes in and that goes out. The source of his life is another and this causes the breath to flow.' So I try to feel not that the breath is something made by me but that IT breathes in me. And It, the soul, the Atman, and Brahma are the same, and it put me here and takes me back on its lap. We lie, says Emerson, in 'the lap of a great intelligence'.

There has to be, then, something more than the seven mad gods because God cannot be more unconscious than I am. There must be a greater consciousness than I am and if God is both immanent and transcendent then there must be an immanent consciousness, a greater potential for consciousness than I can visualize at this moment. 'As from a fire-flame thousands of sparks come forth, even so from the Creator an infinity of beings have life and to Him return again,' says the Mundaka Upanishad. A friend of mine whose brother died in an airplane accident said she dreamed, the very night she heard of the disaster, that he came to her and said, 'I like this place I am in.' Well, Nirvana is the place where strivings end and hope is not and nothing is, except loss of self in the all—but this is not according to Hoyle in the Game of Life that we westerners play.

I know what the Upanishads are saying, that there are moments of identity with the all, here and now, timeless moments, that a few wise sages are privileged to have, and this is their bliss. I can think it. I can feel it shadow-like, as a dim sensation. I can imagine myself IN the tree, the bird, the lotus in the fish pond.

But somehow it is all anti-climax. And the seven mad gods dance on, while we poor human fragments, floating on the sea of God's unconsciousness, try to make our peace with words like 'transcendent' and 'immanent'.

THREE JOURNAL EXCERPTS, DECEMBER, 1955

For the past three weeks, but particularly the past week, I have not been feeling well. I am tired when I wake up in the morning and tired in the evening, although I have tried to take it easy. After meals, I feel rumblings and gurglings in and around the pancreatic area and occasionally, particularly when I lie in bed in the late evening, I feel a dull, slight pain there. My urine and my stools have been abnormal. I have not gained any weight as far as I know since the operation, and I 'feel thin'. There seems to be a loss of strength since October and November. Although I have tried very hard to think on the positive side of things and not let the doctor's predetermined time of one year, of which six months have gone by, preclude all the possibilities, these symptoms certainly darken the *joie de vivre* with which I would like to confront life in this critical year.

Now there can be a number of explanations. The cancer is spreading and beginning to encroach on new areas ahead of the doctor's prognostication. If I have what he described as a slight chance of a 'bizarre form of pancreatitis' then it is either getting worse or going away, in the latter case with a few final fireworks before the final exit. I could have a mild case of intestinal flu, which I have had occasionally in the past. I could still be disturbed by psychic forces set loose after my problem with John.

[*See chapter III*]. If it is the masculine side calling to me, I have certainly tried to act upon it and do note a change in my attitudes and actions, despite the general debility. I am willing to thrust my jaw out like a man and take what comes, even though it means pressing my limited energy.

I am in the difficult position of not knowing what the next minute, the next hour, the next day, the next month will bring. The possibilities of life or illness or death are all equal, one shading into the other, as the future unrolls like a carpet under my feet. I am literally suspended, as it were, in the eternity of flux and much more keenly aware of my sense-relationship with the immediate moment than I have ever been. It is true that I could go to the doctor for a check on these symptoms. I am also in the difficult position of trying to determine the hair-breadth line between what is physiological and what is psychical. In analysis also one can have symptoms of these kinds, attendant upon deep changes within one's self.

But I see no point at the moment, or at least until after Christmas holidays, in hitting the M.D's. for an answer. I was given the prognosis and invited to come in any time. If the prognosis is true then what I am having could be expected. A cancer patient does not really recover and some of these symptoms, lack of weight, debility, are naturally to be expected. If it is something else, time and faith will reveal the change and a brighter horizon. I want all of me to think of that latter possibility and to believe in it, but I am again and again reminded that I am essentially involved in what can only be a religious problem.

It occurred to me last night that I have been working too much alone on this problem. My analyst, of course, has given wonderful help in encouraging me to hold all in suspension, to believe in all possibilities, and to help me find deep roots within my real Self that will nourish and sustain me. Ruth's kindly hand as we share my changing feelings together is always there to grasp mine. It is a friendly and warm hand and I am sure now I am more related to her than to anyone I have ever known. 'But now,' I said to myself, 'I must turn to The Other One, He who is far greater than I, and yet He who has part of Him in me.' For a little bit the universe lighted up, as though someone had flicked a switch in a darkened room. I saw myself really for what I am, a human being, a member of a species of which I am inordinately proud, who for a time here played a part in the drama of human experience. My omissions and commissions I saw clearly and, although there have been many omissions I was not too anxious about them. We see as through a glass darkly, always. I have at least tried to see, dark as my vision often was. I have communicated a spirit to others which was also in me. I have run away, or bottled life up in compartments, but there are also many times when I have embraced this life, the most precious of all gifts, warmheartedly and openly. For this I am proud.

Now by 'calling on the Other One,' I mean that I am going to have to put my trust in larger forces at work around me than I can see now. We are all infinitely small in the face of God and the infinite purposes of the universe. Yet little as we are beside the Tremendum, we are not excluded. Whether my cancer be real or imaginary, whether the firefly glow of myself be extinguished now or twenty years from now, I am not excluded. It is only the man who has turned his back on life that excludes himself from the continuous creation of the universe. The Other One is the larger than me and yet the deepest in me. It is what, if I give myself to It, can bend and stretch me to Its purposes. And, in so doing, I can figuratively lay many of my cares and worries upon the lap of this Other One who shares with me the co-creation of my life.

There is an important distinction here, as the spider-web of destiny is crisscrossed by gossamer filaments that must be discriminated out with sensitivity. I am not saying, I hope, that I resign myself to whatever comes, in the mood of being tortured by a horrible fate, or by a fatal fascination to a death-wish. It is true that back there three years ago, in my garden, about four in the afternoon, when I had been drinking some sherry and I wished I hadn't, I said to myself, 'If you don't give this up you will pull the house down, as you did with Margaret.' There was a possible death-wish and guilt-command in that statement, but I would prefer now to see it for what it was, one of those random fantasies that occur to all human beings in their darker, guilt-ridden moments. If one gave one's self up to all the fantasies that come to one's life, one would be back with the primitives, circumscribed by a terror world of ghosts and demons and taboos.

But our increased consciousness, lying close, if we can let it, to the vast unconscious universe that we each carry as our life-line to universal psychic energy, can help us to distinguish more subtly what is to be feared and what not to be feared. With me, by saying that I am resigning myself to the Other One, I am putting it in the affirmative: 'Thy will be done.' Tomorrow will take care of itself. I may wake up tired tomorrow. Or I may wake up fresh with energy. I am not going to worry about it. The Other One holds in his hands my Karma and this I must trust. And when I am sick in spirit I can put my hand out in the darkness, particularly my left hand, for that is my unused side, and ask Him to grasp it. Judging from last night's experience of the Other, lightness and freedom can come from this loving trust. After all, my anxieties have to do with mechanical time, a man-made invention, 8 o'clock classes to teach, 6 o'clock dinner, bed at 11 o'clock and so forth. His time is organic and psychic, the rhythms in nature and the rhythms in me. If I put my trust in these rhythms, I will let Him lead me. Who knows what to-morrow will bring? And who cares? It is *now* that I am typing this and *now*, as I look out the window, that the redwood tree is green-growing in the winter sunshine and, though Pippa is not passing with what I have always regarded as·her silly song, God is indeed in the universe.

*   *   *

Legitimate guilt is for not doing what one sees to do. For-giveness is going on from where we are, moving forward. 'Son, thy sins are forgiven, Arise, take up thy bed and walk.' We cannot assume God is an oaf.

*   *   *

Christmas Eve, 1955: I went to bed imagining God's hands working over my body, and it gave me considerable comfort. I kept saying, 'Bless me, God.' The hand seemed to make me feel better, especially the unseen part that kneaded me within. I had a real feeling He was my creator.

Reading Brennin's book on Dylan Thomas in America gave me real joy. What a creative character, despite the retching and vomiting! He could really live in the now—except when the dark spells came.

136

THE LARGER MEANINGS

FIVE JOURNAL EXCERPTS, JANUARY, 1956

New Year 1956: Live now as though each day were to be enjoyed for itself—the people, the colours, the moods, the intimate acquaintances with my family—and hope that each day will bring some manna for my well being. As the prayer says—'Our daily bread.' Do not be afraid to think occasionally of the future I had expected but will not have. It induces sorrow and tears which are good, and these tears can sometimes become tears for the universe, sorrow for mankind—for as Ecclesiastes says, 'There is a time. . . .'

*　　　*　　　*

God, this the New Year is the turning year for me, turning as the leaves turn, turning as the earth turns, turning as man turns, and this is the year in which I am to walk in the valley of the shadow where all mystery lies. Let me enter then upon the ledger of my hopes and fears a word or two about whatever sacrifice I will be called upon to make. This may be the year of supreme sacrifice, the giving up of my life. Frankly, I do not understand why this should have to be an immanent possibility now. I must distinguish between voluntary and involuntary sacrifice, and also the sacrifice of what I can conceive of my highest opportunity and values. Sacrifice is giving up later meaning. I give myself to Your keeping but give myself as I am.

I have questions of God. Does my personal sacrifice enlarge You? If I see I have a task to do, do I help God to know Himself better because I have the capacity to know myself better? Is that the point where I choose to sacrifice my independence for a divine interdependence? Why do I react not cosmically but personally, here in me? It is I that is being hurt. What are some of the elements in sensing the Tremendous? What happens with the miracle? The surprise is when God seems to step out of His law, irrationally, positively, absurdly. 'Whatever happens is God's will' is an orthodox Christian position; the study of Jesus' teachings helped me through that. What happens *isn't* God's will, but God's will is what I do with what happens. There must be meaning in it. I don't understand all of God's laws. Out of darkness things come not known to Him. Responsibility is ability to respond, and if we experience interaction, no matter what the source, what we have to do is respond. More and more

I enter into it, I am committed. Responsibility is every motion, every action that happens. Am I really helping His unfinishedness? The miracle being, do I change Him as I change? So the divine and humble arrogance—is it possible that what I do is important to Life, if I keep knocking long enough? Jesus faced the cross voluntarily. He could have left but he didn't. The only question is, how voluntarily am I meeting it?

*　　　*　　　*

The most important things we can bring to prayer are our imperfections. Imperfection is one thing God really needs. Voluntarily to bring our imperfections is hard to do! To bring our most dark and imperfect side, the only side we risk in being human! Christianity has not incorporated His dark side in images of man or of God.

I know that nothing can be done over again; that these imperfections are done, but that they are the necessary stumbling parts that make up the warp and woof of my many-threaded experience. I meditate on these stumbling wrong decisions as I learn more about my opposites. I must bend and yield, in the spirit of Laotze, to the impulses of God in the universe, but at the same time be aware of the need to 'wrestle with the angel,' the sleeping side of God. I resolve to have courage and hope—to live as long as I can, and not be defeated when giving in completely to the deep sleep.

*　　　*　　　*

Now I have read books on prayer, like Gerald Heard's *Preface to Prayer*, with his discussion of the three levels, prayer for one's self, prayer for others, and high prayer as the petitionless affirmation of God's will. Sometimes, in a state of low petitionary prayer, I simply ask for a miracle. Or for myself to forget myself and pray for the family, but then that involves myself. Or pray for all people seen and not seen who are faced with the extremity of cancer. Sometimes I think I approach a state of mind somewhat near Jesus at Gethsemane: 'Sit ye here, while I go yonder and pray . . . my soul is exceeding sorrowful, even unto death; abide ye here and watch with me.'

And he went forward a little and fell on his face, and prayed, saying, O my Father, if it be possible, let this cup pass away from me: nevertheless, not as I will, but as thou wilt.

I am but a speck in the massive face of the universe, like a mote against the massive rib of the High Sierra. Yet God, who includes all, must care, for He is inside me and outside me. The miracle I ask for may not mean a removal of the burden within, though I must keep this also in the realm of possibilities, since He is all-inclusive. If I put my trust in his thrust—the word 'thrust' suggesting a life power not implicit in the word 'trust' —perhaps I can complete myself and in such a way as He could say, 'This too, is my Son in whom I am well pleased.'

My religious problem—for all desperate situations are religious problems—has been that of distinguishing between my felt experience as a unique human being, and the generalized language of prayer, between feeling and idea, between what I was supposed to say and what I really felt. I begin to discern the real meaning of the protestant experience of the individual alone before God. The Giver of Life would respect that, more than formalized patterns of words or doctrines. A man is a tree, with roots in the earth, branches in the sky. And a redwood tree cannot be an oak or a myrtle.

And so I evolve little prayers of my own in my own language, sometimes in poetry like the following:

> I know who you are, God.
> How could I have ever forgotten?
> You are the wind at the gate of the year
> And the song in the heart of the lark
> The neap tide of the new year
> And the ebb of silence.

Or with formal prayer this yearning to close the gap between my own personal felt-experience, my own background of learning, and the imposed 'church words' lead to a rendering of the Lord's Prayer with my own connotations for each word. The connotations differ, as I meditate on each word, but they tend to run something like this:

'Our Father who art in heaven.' Father is the giver of life within me. He is also mother, not a personal father and mother but the kind referred to by Thomas Wolfe when he speaks of the subject of all his fiction as 'man's search for his father,' the source of his personal meaning. Father is the Sky-Father of the Navajos and the Great Earth-Mother, the archetypal figures inwardly at work in all human beings, and whose outlines are clearly discerned in religion and myth. Fully taken into my experience from that long ago of 1949 is Margaret's last dream, of a Great Baker, kneading the dough of humanity into loaves of bread. Thus I cannot exclude the forgotten language of dreams, now freshly evoked by my own crisis, from my religious orientation.

'Heaven' cannot be the literal sky. I know too much about the vast interstellar spaces opened to modern man by astronomy to accept the confident Dantean view of the cosmos, with the earth at the centre of revolving creation. 'Heaven' can be that mysterious inner Kingdom which is the realization of the ego, the uniting of conscious and unconscious, and the uniting of God with one's oneness. As for 'heaven' in a life after death, I have a number of theories to choose from. However, as I tell myself, I can well adopt the attitude of Henry David Thoreau who, on his deathbed, when asked if he had any vision of the other world, replied, 'One world at a time, sir, one world at a time.' Asking now about immortality would be like asking a seven-year-old whether he preferred Hamlet or Macbeth. And I am still very much of a child in a spiritual kindergarten.

With the word 'Father,' I keep trying to feel strength and courage; with 'Mother,' sensitivity, feeling. I realize at once a play of active and passive in me, an aggressive thrust and a feeling return. Only the two are one in one—two principles that seem at the time to govern my being. Then I say, 'Who art in heaven,' and try to feel into 'Thy kingdom is within us!' I try to feel out the nature of this kingdom not yet attained within. A kingdom is a country ruled by a sovereign. The kingdom is unique in me, but I feel my work in the kingdom of myself enhanced through the kingdom of others. . . . The kingdom I am seeking is very still, as though everything were moving around it but in the centre there was no motion; it is a land of lost content. One does not reach it by striving. It comes by no-striving. It is a garden—I am sure of that for me; the nature of the garden is just beyond my glimpse.

'Hallowed be thy name' recalls the original Anglo-Saxon meaning of 'holy,' 'whole'. To be holy was to be whole. For 'whole' I can write in 'all-inclusive,' for God to me includes everything in the universe. As a Christian, I rebel against excluding other kinds of religious experience. Like Walt Whitman, I can exclude nothing from God. What is 'holy' is 'whole,' and my illness and my analysis have certainly demonstrated to me shadow sides of myself, incomplete sides, that must be rectified. These are my sins, my omissions, and, through use of these, I can redeem them. This can make me whole or holy in God's sight.

'Thy Kingdom come, Thy will be done, on earth as it is in heaven.' If the coming kingdom is that which made for wholeness in me, then God will be pleased in this, his son. I can at this point in the prayer only stumble to find words for this dynamic concept: The kingdom within where Self is merged in God is the Kingdom where man and God are one . . . the really creative self is always in emergence in all human beings, and death occurs in us every day for we must die into the new . . . Kingdom-come is that merging on earth of one's identity with the great current of life. And when 'in heaven,' one gives one's life to the broad flowing river that disappears on the horizon of all mortal creatures. 'On earth' is the sparrow flitting joyously in the sun. 'In heaven' is the sparrow who disappears on the horizon into the meeting of earth and sky.

'Give us this day our daily bread, and forgive us our trespasses as we forgive those who trespass against us.' Forgiveness means starting anew, because one is forgiven what he has done. And, as we would forgive ourselves, we forgive our neighbours. We can wipe the slate clean of anxieties and doubts, and 'enter heaven as little children' by starting afresh with awe and reverence and surprise before the changing face of life.

'Lead us not into temptation but deliver us from evil,' means that God gives us choices. We are asking Him to help us make the right choices. I can never accept the deterministic God of the Puritans nor of logical positivism. Nor can I accept a collectionist universe made up of blind chance. For me there is free will and therefore possibility and therefore purpose. I have always been fond of Melville's famous chapter, 'The Matmaker' in *Moby Dick*. It conveys exactly how I feel about the relation of what is determined to what is free choice—to what is chance. The warp of the loom, the fixed threads, is the given, what I had at birth. I cannot rebel against this. The woof is the element of freedom, what I can choose to weave into the warp. And I have certainly chosen a good deal, faced with many alternatives. The darkskinned weaver with his knife, uncertainly pushing each thread of the woof into place, is the element of chance; and I do not know exactly where the thread will rest.

*　　　*　　　*

Finally, the 'Our daily bread' partly resolves itself into a third kind of personal rendition of the Lord's Prayer:

> Our heavenly Father and our Mother in earth
> Sky and sea, land and leaf commingled
> Hallowed, hallowed be thy name.
>
> When the silent dove is singled
> Swallowed in thy tongue of flame
> Fire and bird, earth and sky are one.
>
> Thy kingdom come, thy will be done
> As the runneled hills are still
> Where the fountains and the rivers run.
>
> And life and death join together
> On the lip of thy horizon
> In song of praise for thy communion.
>
> Give me, this day, my bread O Lord
> That I may share in what you have stored
> Thy hand shape round this daily loaf.
>
> Here on earth as in heaven
> Take it, bake it, in my oven
> That I may taste thy leaven.
> Forgive my debts as I forgive those
> Who, unknowing, see my darkened heart
> And take the bramble for the rose.
>
> And lead me not unto temptation
> To mistake the rind for the fruit
> Where good from evil I may choose.
>
> For this is Kingdom, Kingdom come
> Kingdom unKinged in transformation
> By thy crucible of lambent flame.

Father, Mother, Earth, Sky
'Amen' with the muted temple gong.

'Amen' end my prayer and song.

Who can ask about tomorrow if he has his daily bread? For each of us is transformed every moment, whatever the cause and effect—and what is cause and what is effect but two candles lighted on our two feet here to there, yesterday to today, and today to tomorrow. If God's presence is in this moment, which is a no-time-moment because He is eternal, then how can I deliberately cultivate this sense of presentness?

This 'sense of presentness' Mark did most courageously cultivate during his final weeks. He knew in his deepest being that time was drawing away from him, although he held before himself again and again the possibility of temporal existence. His physical body relentlessly harried him with miseries which, because he could not ignore, he included under God. Finally the surgeon decided on a second operation—and from this point on, as evidenced in the letters and in the journal excerpts, Mark began to pull his life's threads into a single design.

LETTER TO ANALYST, APRIL, 1956

I would like to share this with you. Yesterday was quite an agonizing day for me but today I feel quite calm and resigned. You see I was unduly optimistic when you so kindly came down, with that wonderful creativity. To speak of sewer matters, which are as much a part of God as sunsets and heart-throbs, my urine is dark again and my jaundice and the itch are worse. I discovered by experimenting that it is occasionally light after I have drunk a lot of water, thereby flushing out something, but it is dark again particularly when I have food digested. The doctor says that as soon as there is no indication of bacteria in the blood stream they will do another operation. The last X-rays, he positively states, would not indicate a spread of malignant tumor elsewhere, but (1) there could be a closing of the shunt as a result of malignancy in the pancreas, or (2) a stoppage, in some other way, of the shunt or duct. I do feel we should face every possibility. Stare hard at whatever reality is and face the fact that I may have to face a final transformation which I say is a losing of one's life to save it in the final sense. After opening me up they may discover there is not much they can do. Or whatever they do may be just a temporary stopgap. Now we have struggled hard together on the 'work' and it has been a wonderful experience for me. I think we both tacitly understood that we were talking about two things in our many hours together. A transformation, the coming of a new man, whether here or as a part of the ultimate giving of one's self which we call death, in view of the eternal mystery is a going back to God, or a fusing of my life with on-going life that none of us will ever quite be able to compel. Krutch's Anthology was just right for me, particularly his introduction and his magnificent selections from Thoreau. I never realized how much was in the notebooks that I don't recall reading in *Walden's Pond*. Particularly I liked the stories of my 'fishy friend,' his account of his enjoyment in being with the bream, and also the part about the loon. I suddenly realized how all living matter is connected or blended into the life stuff— whatever you want to call it. And in a sense how my death, when it comes, is a going back home into that eternal creation of life stuff from which man, as well as the fishy friend and the loon, comes.

Many other symbols have evolved and fallen into place. For example, when no one was around the house for a while, when I was completely alone, I cried in the kind of 'agony'—I use the word with the Greek connotation—and as I looked at myself in the mirror I felt that God was crying too. I mean by this that I felt I was reflecting the eternal sorrow of the universe that is part of God, just as joy is a part of God and a reflection of His image. To die at my age, and mind you I haven't given up hope, is a kind of martyrdom. I mean not so much that it can be a transforming experience for those around me, but that to yield my life to redeem it is in itself an experience that at the moment I cannot find the words for. Celia in *The Cocktail Party* deliberately chooses the way of death as a voluntary sacrifice. Mine is involuntary but no less real. Yes, miracles can happen, but I really do feel I should be prepared for the other possible contingency. I am sending this off in the hope you will get it before the phone call. Let us still hope together, but let us also consider the possibility of a final transformation, hard as it is for all of us to face.

Mark.

ANALYST'S REPLY TO PREVIOUS LETTER

Dear Mark,

Your letter came this afternoon, and I was deeply moved and impressed by your expression of what is happening to you. Yes, of course, we have been and are now together going into the unknown labyrinth of transformation at all levels, and holding all possibilities open. Whatever else the opus may involve, it does involve finding Life, in the most basic and fundamental meaning of Life. As Jesus knew and found Life, and as he believed each of us could also find it. And God is joy and sorrow, and as we live out our heroic task we thus realize God.

I am not yet willing to say death is at hand for you. We cannot know now, and *life* needs our full support. But that this agony, whatever its outcome, is bringing you to a transforming and numinous sense of Self is unquestionable. The diamonds are there, you are finding them every hour.

From a very ancient prayer of St. Augustine, I send these words: 'O Lord, help us to turn to seek Thee; for Thou hast not forsaken Thy creatures as they have forsaken Thee, our Creator. Let us turn and see Thee, for we know Thou art here in our hearts. . . . When we weep in Thy bosom, after all our rugged ways; and Thou dost gently wipe away our tears, and we weep the more for joy; because Thou, Lord, who madest us, doest remake and comfort us.'

Let us hold to this, Mark, and follow where the path leads. God bless you.

My love and faith.

FOUR JOURNAL EXCERPTS DURING THE LAST MONTH, APRIL, 1956

In hospital. And the strength comes from God and God is the supra-personal, the larger than I. And this I requires redemption, either in the crises of the alteration of my living experience, or in the final crisis or change. And what is redemption? The bringing into light of the dark hidden power which seems, to my consciousness, the 'daemon'. Redemption is redeeming the unknown for fuller life, wholeness, completeness. It is a way pointing to Self as near as I can reach it, and this Self is the larger than me and verges on God. For my own act of redemption is also God's destiny.

*   *   *

I have been in bed for three weeks, and for the second time since that first jaundice a year ago this spring which culminated in a serious operation that in itself left me in bed for a month after that. I have never really been sick in my life before; but I nursed my first wife during the period of six months until her death. It is not hard to see then why the very word 'bedridden,' like the word 'cancer,' has almost a traumatic connotation for me. A man is peevish in bed anyway, for his body is in a sense his feminine earth side. I have always, up to last spring, ignored my body, as I have failed to appreciate the earth side of my life, the *materia prima*; as an 'intuitive intellectual' I have spent too much of my life floating in the sky of ideas. Hence I have developed a lopsidedness not uncommon to the professor type. Certainly no wholeness!

All of this is to explain why I feel the need to write myself out. To talk to myself on paper and to capture, as I lie here in bed, not only my changing mood, but all insights that come as I chew the fat of myself.

Right now I feel that every hour is precious, the moments like strings of pearls. Before this I had long hours of despair, and I am trying to rescue myself from the pull back into oblivion, and to find where life is. I must try to monopolize these hours as though I were sole owner of a diamond trust. I have never quite realized before how much of life can be savoured at the moment of time where one is and not dissipated in anxieties about the yesterdays and the tomorrows. Like most of us, I feel that much of my life has been thrown away for the tinsel of ambitious goals and fruitless indirections and delusions. Of course this has been inevitable and unconscious. I would not be what I am if I had not done what I have done. But when one is faced by immediate and possible death, the whole being yearns for the simply human, for the truth of eternity beyond time, eternity that runs a clear stream below the tangled surface.

Since this latest illness, although I have had some comfort from sporadic reading, I have had a revulsion against books. Books are my business. But now I find more pleasure in looking out the window at the garden, or in the expression on the faces of the

146

children. One burst into the room in a spin of delight, one grabbed at my pen shouting, 'I want to kiss you'. One arrived after dinner to play an hour of poker with me. One bounced in the air because he just received a prize in a speech contest. The dog in furry delight sneaked into the bedroom to lick my big toe, and finally my wife touched my hand as she said, 'Good night,' to give me strength and courage, for she is the one who can really take it and keep her head above water. Such rich delights are of a different kind from what I am used to.

I lie and remember such things as a waddling turtle, a chipmunk with his pouch full of nuts, a golden trout leaping high on the river—and suddenly I realize what life is, for lichen, turtle, or man—we share together the moving experience that is the ceaseless river of life and we must learn the ritual of this eternal river and not be betrayed by the artificiality of the clock. Clock time is relatively a recent invention, an abstraction. The mechanical clock, curiously enough, was a religious device invented by monks in the twelfth century to help them keep their devotions to God. When the clock became secular our western civilization began. Industrialism and capitalism would not have been possible without a notion of mechanical time. Specialization piled upon specialization to give birth to our present complex inter-meshed machine age society, and if each man did not time himself with every other man in this web of specialism, urban life would fall apart in one or two days.

The clock makes the world we live in possible, and one would not deny that we have reached far these past fifty years in raising the creative comforts of the masses. But we can also be betrayed by the clock; perhaps I am more conscious of this fact than most people. If there is to be an ultimate transforming End for me soon, the clock will not be there.

There are moments, for I am a human being, when I envy others who reckon upon a 'natural life span'. This is unfair! God, how could you do this to me? Why? Why? Why? Few others have been given this final transformation in the middle of life, or so the newspapers tell us. What is happening to me is what happens when a lethal parasite destroys a sturdy tree. Nor can I expect God suddenly to reverse His natural laws He set up at the beginning, for I am enough a pupil of our age of science to know that. It would be unfair to ask God arbitrarily to shift the order of the universe, bode it ill or be it good. There are miracles, too. I have not fallen into despair. I have found the strength beyond hope and despair and this strength comes from a faith in letting things happen whichever way the cards turn. Some might call this 'yielding to God's will'. In the Navajo myth the heroes in search of their father would say, 'Well, we will know where we are going when we get there.'

One of my most difficult problems this past year has been that of distinguishing between the official language of the established Christian churches as against trying to realize a genuine religious experience that was felt from the heart. We are told we are going through a period of religious revival. Americans are supposed to be flocking back to the churches. They relinquished them for golf and picnics on Sundays in the 1920's; mass man is now developing an interest in religion appropriate to what Toynbee calls a 'time of troubles'. This is not to be decried; a brush with religious experience gives direction to the age of mass delusion. It can, however, protect man from the school of personal spiritual wrestling. Mass Man is not ready for dealing directly in his deeper self with the dimension of personal meaning.

For the aware person the way is both more difficult and more rewarding; one is much more conscious, more like a harp receiving impulses from the kingdom of heaven within, more aware of that mystery I call the chain of being, more sensitive of what it means to be transformed. One is closer to one's self. On the other hand the personal journey is more difficult. Searching into self for wholeness is no easy road. The labyrinth is dark and is blocked by falls, turns, and dead ends. We who have the 'experience in depth' are like strangers in an unfamiliar city trying to find the right house on a nameless street and no filling station to give us a free map for the asking. We pay a price. Any real effort costs something. Counterfeit money is exchanged for real money. Gorgons lie waiting, and one must be ever alert with no magic word that will carry him forward to where the minotaur is that must be slain. It is best to take along a helper, as Dante took Virgil, or as Ariadne was invoked as the guide with the golden thread.

The reward? One is closer to one's self, one perceives the full dimension of the spirit. Microcosm to macrocosm, self to Self, the part to the greater whole that is God. Since man with his consciousness is part animal, part angel, this is the only way that the irreconcilable opposites can be brought together.

Last night I felt I was growing weaker, sicker. At the same moment I realized, as I have before of late, that I was in God's hands. They were warm loving hands that caressed me from my head to my toes. The eternal wrestle with the ambiguous nature of mere words makes it difficult to describe this experience. For words represent only a minutiae of human experience, even in great poets like Dante or Eliot. Yes, it is 'a terrible thing to fall into the hands of the living god'. And as with all words, one must evoke for these the connotations that personally match the language of a far distant time. It is an awesome thing, a numinous experience, to genuinely feel God's presence within. The intelligent scientist can find an ultimate purpose in the universe and call it evolution. The orthodox Christian can abase himself, imitate a Jesus Christ and make the agony into an object of devotion, and can then rest assured he is 'saved'. But to feel God as an urgent inner experience, right here and now—well—that is something else altogether! What the final transformation of one's self to the larger God self is, no one knows. Certainly not Billy Graham, or Harry E. Fosdick, or even Reinhold Niebuhr. Maybe the mystics know. Maybe C. G. Jung has premonitions. For they have been deeply aware of the personal journey. Experiencing the kingdom within is certainly not orthodox, and probably has always been unique with every seeking individual depending upon what he brings to the experience. Certainly the depth achieved by the search is of extreme importance if one is to die and not feel that this dying is all very remote from one's self.

Perhaps death is a going on to the life out of which we came. Certainly it doesn't involve joining in the dismal futility of seeing Uncle Joe or Aunt Ellie beyond the pearly gates kept by St. Peter—not for our very conscious twentieth century. Who can know fully the mystery of the river of life out of which we come —keeping our heads above water for a time—and back to which we go—not to drown but to bathe in the sublime? Death is veiled in shadows by God, and obviously in His own design, or we would become arrogant supermen. Perhaps also death is life for those around us. Which brings me, since I am meditating on large meaningful questions here (and the questions, the eternal questions themselves are more satisfying than the cheap fifteen-cent-store answers)—which brings me to the question of what is life for? To start with, isn't hell a negation of life, a refusal to grow spiritually, a deep freeze of life? As for the meaning in life, at this point I can see things with an astonishing clarity as I never could before. My first tendency when I was given a year to live last July was to blame myself for my sins, for the terrible ways in which I prevented life from ever becoming. I could catalogue these 'sins' over pages of manuscripts. But they are really unimportant.

Life is growth towards fulfilment of self. Much of the wrong we do to others and to our own egos is unconscious. There should be no words like 'sin' or 'guilt' connected with it, unless one uses these words after the fact, as it were, as a goad to enlargement of self. The straightened and narrow gate is only open to those who have encountered the living God, learned the lessons of eternal love, that key word enscribed over the doorway of eternity. The narrow gate is open only to those who are able to forgive their so-called sins by realizing that these were necessary solvents in the transforming process. The realization of this, it seems to me, is the realization of the Centre of being. Obviously a different centre for every human being, but always the same no matter in what way it is worded. We must all strive for uniqueness, for how else can God work but by infinite variation. Yes, I should have done this or that, but I wouldn't be here now cherishing this insight if I hadn't done what I have done. Isn't this really what it means to say' 'I accept myself'?

*   *   *

Meditation on the way things are: How do I stand now at this point of my sickness? What is the relation of what is happening to me to a larger meaning? What problems do I need to confront myself with, in order to make the transformation of Self a complete one? I have grown, or rather diminished, to mere skin and bones, terribly thin. My severe jaundice with the accompanying bile drip indicates there is something terribly wrong inside. Nor do little abrasions, two or three cuts and pimples, heal quickly. The things that people tell me to give me a ray of hope do not always hitch together and I have had ups and downs. I am hungry a good deal but do not put on weight though I eat heartily as though I were nourishing an enemy in my body. The technique for cancer patients is to keep alive a ray of hope but I am suspicious and suspect that 'they' are withholding the truth from me.

Now everyone is with me in my clinging to the ray of hope. Ruth refuses to take the dark side of it, quite naturally. My analyst has held all along to the possibility of an irrational side of things, and says that I darken things more than I need to. If the psyche or soul has an independent life of its own apart from the soma, or if the psyche and soma mirror each other in some way, then not only the ray of hope but psychosomatic factors should be brought into the picture. The mechanist would dismiss all this as nonsense, for to him dreams and imagination and the high aspirations of man are but the result of chemicals interacting in the body. The faith healer would deny the presence of the body and thus fail to recognize the facts of reality. People do have unfortunate accidents. There is cancer in the world. There can be imaginary cancer, as the famous case Jung cites in *Psychology and Religion*. There can also be real cancer, for my first wife had it, ánd my own eyes saw the X-rays of the lungs, and witnessed the whole painful course to the end. Somewhere, in between, lies the truth.

I am on the threshold of startling insights and an experience that should contribute much, not only to solve my egocentricity, but to illuminate some of the plaguey problems that threaten our distraught century. There are particular insights that have to do with sharpening the meaning of Toynbee's discovery of experience in depth, 'withdrawal for renewal,' and my firm belief that the current issues of the time can be resolved by Jung's discovery that science as a statement of 'nothing-but' the reduction to simple elements excludes the complexity in man's soul and therefore renders only partial truth. The observed facts are surely much more complex and all-embracing than a limited scientific logical positivism stemming only recently from the eighteenth century enlightenment. Jung's broadness of scope appeals to me as an historian of ideas.

Most important, this unfortunate turn of events seems to leave my family in the middle, like a deep cut through a half-grown tree. Ruth has a tremendous responsibility and needs a husband and guide. The girls are nearly three years old and even now they are displaying increased need for a father. Eric is graduating from high school, and since I am college professor I could guide him through the difficult years. John is going to high school this coming fall, and these are years in which a father is definitely needed.

On the other hand, my sudden death may not be a disaster but a mysterious and positive element in their growth. Life does take over, and life, realized by people as able as those in my family, can heal. Formerly disparate elements can be fused into a new and vital unity, as a result of my own ultimate experience. Now I see the boys always at odds with each other; they may discover a real kinship in themselves. The boys love the little girls and all of them may grow immeasurably by this sorrowful experience. Our burden is heavy this past year, but Ruth too has discovered a new sense of responsibility, and a femininity she did not have before. She has deepened as a woman, been 'selected,' as it were, for the purpose of finding a deeper meaning in the universe than has been allotted to most of us. If the purpose of life is to find and give meaning, to discover the real love of the world and not the frustrating false love of egocentricity and the slippery masks, well, then Ruth has hit upon it.

How closely numinous symbols come together! Jesus dying on the lowly cross, on which criminals were punished, is all of us transfigured by death and redeemed in time. He died at the age of thirty-two in the prime of life. Those around him found in themselves a transformation of being as a result of his agony. In the last communion, those to be transformed ate of 'his flesh and blood,' that is, they took on new life as a result of his death. Isn't each one of us, particularly those of us who honestly feel we have been 'chosen'—what I call the unlucky-lucky ones—participants in this eternal process of death and transformation? By our deaths are others nourished and given added life and meaning?

Who am I to say in this great mystery in which all human beings are enshrouded that this is not the purpose of God calling me in the middle of life, harsh as it seems, unfair as it sometimes appears. I do not know about the children, but the discovery of real and genuine relationship may help the others, my family and some of my close friends, to undergo partial transformations themselves and be nourished by my facing of my destiny. If the kingdom of heaven is within, then is not this truth closely related to it, an intimate part of it? However, in a world in which God or purpose manifests itself by the play of opposites, I still hold to the possibility that the direct yielding up of myself to the greater thing that is God may not be asked. Another possibility would be that I have been brought to the brink of death for a larger purpose in this world, and that if I regard closely my body, and work hard upon my psyche to bring it to completion, by ferreting out the causes, somatic and psychic, of my present condition, I can survive this crisis for further activity in this world of time.

This thought raises a host of questions. How can I establish more relatedness with my family (for the more related I am to them the more life pulls me to life rather than an abyss of negativity?) Why do I feel that everyone is conspiring against me to withhold the facts on my cancer? That the doctors who are usually so straightforward in their approach, are cooking up fabrications in their alternatives, and frankly admit they are puzzled although I feel they are in a conspiracy? That my analyst knows the truth but is holding out a ray of hope dishonestly instead of really believing there are alternate possibilities? Whence come these feelings that everything is not really to be trusted, that all is illusion? My faith, my beliefs, my imagination, my soul, the whole construction of my life that gives it meaning? That actually there is nothing, nothing at all, that life is an illusion? I participate here in the common problem of twentieth century man, but there is a more personal source for this basic distrust of life, and from what part of my difficult childhood experience does this spring? All of these things require separate meditations for no other purpose than that I should discover the truth about myself, and the truth shall set me free. To my mechanistic friends all this examination will seem morbid, but there is a vast difference between introspection and introversion; if life is to have meaning it must have personal meaning. Existence on the shallow surface of things can be an escape from reality, and reality is deep within our natures. By experience in depth we become whole, and wholeness for each of us is the only solution, in our fragmented century, to pull us through our time of troubles. If we are whole within, life can partake of this wholeness which we bring to it.

* * *

Meditation on Trust and Distrust:

I go back to the hospital tomorrow night for a second exploratory operation. All last evening I spent staring at an old Chinese mandala; what a tremendous effect it has on me! The TV set came. I played poker with the boys, and did nonsense cutouts with the girls, and really felt a relationship between us. I wrote a meditation and ended with a basic question that was answered a few hours later. The surgeon called and said he wanted an exploratory right away; before, he had said two weeks more.

Now this raised the whole question, evidently a basic one with me deep in my psyche, of my trust in people, and, even more vital, in myself. I had really believed he was stalling things because I was a hopeless case. Now the operating may turn out useless but the mere fact he wants to operate is a hopeful sign. He was not 'kidding' me along by giving me the truth when he said there were three possibilities. The point is, I didn't believe him. I even felt he was getting me in the hospital to end me, or to force me to spend my last days away from home. My suspicions then were groundless. I have even felt that my analyst and my wife were 'hiding things' from me when they weren't. They had trust in my possible recovery. Why did I have a basic feeling that beyond the beyond there is nothing at all? That faith and trust are illusions, the facts are—there is nothingness? So here is much to chew on and digest.

At home I have discovered of late that when my mask is off— the mask that makes me so charming at school—I only half listen to the members of my family. I am really not related to their own needs and problems when I am masked, but tend to get preoccupied with books, big plans, and ideas, my school work. I do not feel into the 'now' of the moment. This whole terrible thing that is happening to me is a further turn of the screw. I keep thinking it is an awesome thing to look into the face of the living God. I feel God is turning the screws so I will get into an ultimate position of transition, but I also feel that the centre of the circle is buoying me up, holding me in suspension as though I were in God's hands. And God, terrible and loving, is with me now in His presence.

LAST WRITING HE DID—LETTER TO ANALYST, APRIL, 1956

By the time you receive this I will probably have my exploratory operation. To our great surprise the doctor called up yesterday and said he had made arrangements for me to enter the hospital Sunday and build me up for a Tuesday morning operation. You know me. I had thought he was stalling when he said two weeks from now because he had withheld from me that I was incurable. Evidently this is encouraging. I have much hope. They are genuinely puzzled and want to act right away. There have been moments when I thought you and others were conspiring to withhold the truth and just kidding me along. You can bet I have been working on this problem of basic distrust of others, of a secret conspiracy against me, of any belief in anything, all being illusion, there being nothing. The feeling that no matter how well things were going consciously, my unconscious would react negatively. I wrote pages and pages of recall yesterday. Indeed, the news from the doctor came shortly after I had started working on that as one of my meditations. Whichever way it turns out, I really will not be, as I feel now, cast down. Naturally I want the transformation that would work best for my family, and as I see it that would be living in time. But the ultimate transformation into the river, the broad river of eternal flowing life, I think I am also prepared to accept. You and Elizabeth* certainly know what a person needs. I enjoyed the Eichenberg prints enormously. But it was the Roualt 'Jesus' and the mandalas, particularly the blue one, that were so numinous. I stared at both for what seemed hours. I spent all of last night off and on between sleeps (my itch seems worse) on the mandala. Really it is fascinating but I can't put it into words. In the middle of my staring, a neighbour whom we have gotten to know somewhat came to see me in tears and said she felt I was the only person she could turn to. I spent about two hours with her and she exchanged a confidence in regard to alcoholism and her husband and the effect on her daughter. I asked her to tell me the possible courses of action she could take. They were all escape

* We had given him a series of religious prints by Fritz Eichenberg, a Roualt painting, 'The Holy Face', and a reproduction of a Chinese temple painting.

solutions. Finally I got her into a position where she realized they had to face reality and work out things together, but this had to be done with a helper. So finally she was asking me to suggest an analyst for her particular personality. I gave her the name of one and suggested she call for an appointment. I trust I have done the right thing. But I mention it mostly as a curious part of what has been for me, during the last twenty-four hours, a genuine religious experience. Just a few words about some of the jewels in the dark I have discovered. Because the next time you see me I guess the picture will be altered, and the opposites, at least one pair of them, resolved.

1. I have discovered more than ever before this past week the deeper meaning of family relatedness. I realize now that the charming, effective and 'related-to-others' school teacher was mostly mask. The unmasked real person at home was different, preoccupied, unable really to listen to the heartbeat of the others around him.

2. I have realized that man is arrogant about the other creatures and that they, like man, come from the flowing river and are fellow creatures.

3. I realize I am in God's hands, left and right, and buoyed up on the surface of the infinite by the ocean of God.

4. I realize that in my bumbling way I have given much to other people in their time of need, and I am proud of it, even though I have made many mistakes.

5. I realize that being an intellectual is not really my line. I do not know what my line is yet but I will wait until I get there.

6. I feel quite manly; I am proud of my courage and strength in this encounter.

7. I am quite willing to yield up undue concern about the future to where it belongs, the future. Nor am I concerned about *what I should do*, nor do I feel a sense of guilt or sin about the past, for I wouldn't be where I am, myself as I am, if it hadn't been for that particular past that is mine.

8. The dark malignant powers that seemed to have beset me are not malignant as long as I stare at the mandala and say over and over, 'all is well,' put your trust in unknown, far larger elements than you can ever be completely aware of. The centre is a square, and within, a circle, and within, a curious circular dot, but that is all you write down. The centre is a *tremendum* and a radiant mystery.   Mark.

Epilogue

———◆———

Mark Pelgrin had not yet fulfilled the seasons of God, he was not quite ready for the 'alone journey' to 'the other side where life is,' until his last day was rounded out. It was a soft May morning when, accompanied by Elizabeth Howes, I came to the hospital for a regular visit. Soon we learned that his survival was a matter of a few hours only. We joined his wife and his younger son in his room. And within this small space, antiseptic and impersonal, was contained for seven hours, unceasingly, the clock of time and the unmarked face of eternity.

Outside the room the hospital world moved at its accustomed pace, with its usual sounds of ministration. Inside—what was really there? Did it consist of us who loved him—his friends, his wife with eyes large in grief and shock, his son whose young look was old and patient and beyond itself at that moment? Was it the gaunt and yellowed man, drain tubes strapped to his head and running down his nose, the oxygen mask over his face? Was it Mark Pelgrin himself, looking so intently and remotely into places we could not see? Whatever was there, whoever really came and went during that timeless day, and what emotions rose and fell with the hissing oxygen—who could say with certainty? It was clear only that death and life moved together.

Despite the equipment of medical science surrounding him and participating in his physical existence, Mark was a man, a man filled with dignity. He could not speak; no strength was available for that. But as I came to him, his hand grasped mine and his eyes smiled. 'All shall be well and/All manner of thing shall be well. . . .' The words I said had been a sort of refrain for him during the past week, and he nodded, hearing them, and his lips formed them soundlessly. And those other words I had spoken a week before to tell him that the operation was useless and that his life was over—those words, too, I repeated: 'I said to my soul, be still, and let the dark come upon you/ Which shall be the darkness of God. . . .'

He could not live more than an hour or so, the doctor believed. Mark saw it differently. It was as if all the important persons of his life had to be brought to this point of intersection and departure before his 'time to die' could be embraced. And so it was. During the hours that followed, they came one by one—his parents, a favourite cousin, a sister-in-law, his elder son Eric, his closest friend. Each had, one way or another, played a significant role in Mark's destiny. Each came toward the irrevocable fact of death differently —with fear, with awkwardness, with self-pity, with grief, with love —but always, in some strange way, freely. Such times of stress seem often to be like stained glass windows through which even the feeblest light glows; thus each confrontation had its particular meaning. Some things are sharp in memory still, and poignant. The woman, Ruth, her sensitive face a Dürer engraving of sadness and awe, stroking Mark's forehead and gazing at him with unanswerable questions. Mark's friend Jack grasping both of Mark's hands in his own and saying: 'Mark, I love you!' The immeasurable moment when Eric and John formed a circle of hands with Mark and wept and spoke to their father of love, and of old feuds and reconciliations.

The times between, too, were an ache and a wonder. Three pictures had been with Mark for many days, and all three were in the room —a copy of the compelling Roualt painting, 'The Holy Face,' the mysterious Chinese temple painting, and a large photograph, done by a friend, of a blossoming apple bough against a spring sky. More than once Mark indicated with hand or eyes that he wanted one of these brought closer; and when one of us held them where Mark could see, he seemed to peer into and through them, often nodding his head or moving his lips. Time and space did not exist, so it seemed, but only being—and being was in the centre of a dark circle, or in the stark gaze of 'The Holy Face' meeting the stark gaze of the man on the bed, or in the point of light at the ephemeral tip of an apple branch. Occasionally I spoke to him softly of matters that I knew had concerned him. More often there was an indescribable silence into which the world's noise came muted and alien. Once he asked for a pencil and paper. Slowly and with great effort he drew a circle and then a cross.

'*Do you want a prayer?*' I asked.

He nodded.

'*Our Father which art in heaven. . . .*' The familiar-unfamiliar words closed about us, drew us into a place '*beyond hope and despair*' and held us suspended in the mystery. At the end of the prayer Mark whispered almost inaudibly, '*Everything is a circle*'.

Fingers of fog crept over the coastal hills, the sun edged toward the sea, and Mark Pelgrin's circle closed. As we left the hospital, one son carried some of Mark's clothes, the other, Mark's ever-present briefcase. And I thought of the nurse who said, '*He wants so much to live!*' And of the surgeon who said, '*What a swell guy!*' And the world of people talking, and highways, and gardeners pruning trees, and dogs barking, was unreal.

What did this man accomplish by his dying? He was ordinary, fumbling, always pressed for time, filled with imperfections. He was also extraordinary, not because he was born '*different*' but because, painfully and against great odds, he achieved his own unique truth. By stepping consciously into the centre of his dark circle, he made it more possible for some of us to do likewise when it is our '*time to die*'. He never begged the question of Why and Wherefore during his year of encounter; rather, he opened himself to each question, even the most humiliating, and tried to answer. It was, as he kept saying, '*a terrible thing to fall into the hands of the living God;*' perhaps what his dying accomplished, above all else, was a way of living.

When a man thus '*loses his life,*' not in a physical sense but as a voluntary sacrifice of his most cherished ego defences, he truly finds Life. And '*Religious Statement*' and '*Life Statement*' become one. The seasons of God, Mark believed, must be embraced by man; in so doing, man adds to the consciousness and fullness of God. He accomplished dignity, and the urgent devotion of trying to find the greater meaning behind the paradox of the universe. For any human creature, this is sufficient.

THE THEOSOPHICAL PUBLISHING HOUSE

Wheaton, Ill., U.S.A.

Madras, India   London, England

Publishers of a wide range of titles on many
subjects including:

Mysticism

Yoga

Meditation

Extrasensory Perception

Religions of the World

Asian Classics

Reincarnation

The Human Situation

Theosophy

Distributors for the Adyar Library Series
of Sanskrit Texts, Translations and Studies

The Theosophical Publishing House, Wheaton,
Illinois, is also the publisher of

QUEST BOOKS

Many titles from our regular clothbound list in
attractive paperbound editions

For a complete list of all Quest Books write to:

QUEST BOOKS
P.O. Box 270, Wheaton, Ill. 60187